GRACE

MARY KATHRYN LOVE

Grace be with you, Mary Love

■ HAZELDEN®

Hazelden

Center City, Minnesota 55012-0176

1-800-328-0094

1-612-257-1331 (FAX)

http://www.hazelden.org

Library of Congress Cataloging-in-Publication Data

Love, Mary Kathryn, date.

    Grace / by Mary Kathryn Love.

       p. cm.

    Second work in The Grace trilogy, which the first work was titled Love and the final work was titled Peace.

    ISBN 1-56838-157-3

    1. Love, Mary Kathryn, date—Diaries. 2. Spiritual biography—United States. 3. Love, Grace. I. Title.

    BL73.L68A3 1997

    973.92'092—dc21

                                   97-13288

  [B]   CIP

Cover design by David Spohn

Illustrations by Randy Scholes

Text design by Nora Koch/Gravel Pit Publications

Editor's note

Hazelden offers a variety of information on chemical dependency and related areas. Our publications do not necessarily represent Hazelden's programs, nor do they officially speak for any Twelve Step organization.

Ten percent of the author proceeds from each sale of *The Grace Trilogy* will be donated to The Grace Foundation, an organization established in remembrance of Grace Zuri Love. The Grace Foundation has as its mission *Creating art and sacredness from the ordinary*.

For more information on The Grace Foundation, visit its web site at http://www.gracezurilovefoundation.com

This book is dedicated to two angels:

Gracie
My daughter
This is my gift to You . . .
and
Matthew
My brother
who was there to
greet you when you
arrived.

We speak of writing here, Mary. Let us examine this writing. What is it you want the world to know about your love for your daughter?

That all continues. That love transcends time and space. That I learned so much on this journey with Grace. That I am a better person to myself because of my love for her. That having you and Grace and the Holy Spirit in my life had made it worth living. That we maybe cannot understand all, but that there is a reason for everything. We just may not see it at the time. That love is all there is! I feel it! I am living proof of it!

This is what we speak of here. The freedom to choose not pain but joy! To choose joy! This can be done. Others need to understand that this can be done! You can show them and help them with this lesson, this journey—the journey of choice!

CONTENTS

IN GRATEFULNESS

I could never have made it without the love of my husband, John, who shared this experience of Grace being in our lives. I have never been closer to another human being, as I was to my husband, at the time of Grace's life. We shared something beyond intimacy. There is something we have touched as a couple that will forever be a part of our beings. To him I give my heart.

My love knows no bounds for my stepdaughter, Amanda. Somehow I felt I might not be able to love a child again, but Amanda simply would not let me do it. She knew more about living than I did. I thank her for this every day.

Margaret Perron was the first to see these letters. By gently guiding, and literally blowing dust off the pile of papers I gave her, she helped give this book life, because she believed in it. Margaret led me to Grace. I am forever grateful. Forever.

Julieanne Carver walked with me as a friend, both of us sharing our pregnancies and later the tragedy of Grace's death. In her embracing tenderness, she made me her son Peter's godmother. I love both Julieanne and Kelly, her husband, for this generous gesture.

I thank my mother, Sara Cole, who loved me as only she could, with compassion and a heart that kept me afloat when I thought I would sink and surely drown. I thank my father, Charles Cole, who has always stood by me, every minute—always wanting me to "become" who I needed to be. That time finally came.

I thank Nancy Love, my mother-in-law, for caring for me after Grace's birth. Both Jim and Nancy Love showered us with their compassion. I thank my brother-in-law Peter, for his ability to make me smile, even in the midst of deep grief.

My sister, Liz, never stopped being there for me—from Grace's birth, until the last moments of her life. Liz blessed me with her presence. I thank her husband, Dean, who in his kindness, quietly took care of things that needed to be done. I thank my brother, Charlie, who always made time to talk to me, long distance, always supporting me with his words.

I thank Shirley Koski for tenderly reading this story. I thank Mary Jane Madden, who gave me courage to continue writing, and I thank Debra Kelley, who always was with me in spirit. I thank the nurses and doctors who did all they could for Grace. Especially Sandy, Grace's nurse, who became Grace's second mother. They all loved and fought for her as much as we did. For them I am eternally grateful.

I thank the whole wonderful editorial team at Hazelden Publishing—including Dan Odegard, Steve Lehman, and Caryn Pernu, for bringing this vision to fruition, for believing in life. In particular, I thank my editor, Betty Christiansen, who with her own deep wisdom knew what to do every step of the way with this book. Her spirit is reflected in this work.

My gratefulness extends to my workplace—to Felicia who held me as I cried, to Sheila who always knew what to say, to Fonda's sensitivity, and to my boss, Vernon Weckwerth, who became a father figure to us all, allowing us to grow spiritually, even at work.

And ultimately, I give thanks to my best friend, Debra Bohnen, who dropped everything, day and night, to be by my side, who gently guided me through my pain. Though she is only mentioned briefly in this book, her place in friendship will be forever realized.

N O W

August 1996

The summer heat is beginning to let up, and I know that autumn will soon be here. We live in a working-class neighborhood in St. Paul. There are five homes on our side of the street. We happen to live on the corner. This summer, we have attempted to grow flowers in the backyard, but with the heat, we have seen the grass dry out and the flowers wither. All in all, though, it has been a beautiful summer.

Today I began cleaning our home. I am upstairs, with an old dust rag in my hand. I have made a mental list of all that needs to be done before school begins. For some

1

reason, as fall nears, I want to put the house in order, as if I am getting ready for something. I wonder if this is how people felt in days gone by, as they prepared for the harvest. That is how I feel, as if I am making things ready. I begin to dust.

As I am dusting, I find myself noticing the objects I am picking up. I dust the brass lamps in our bedroom, and I remember how my husband and I had each brought something, each brought a lamp, to our bedroom from our former lives. I thought of how I had bought matching maroon shades for these lamps two years into our marriage, unifying the lamps with color. My lamp is short, my husband's taller with tile work on it. Yet they come together in some type of harmony now. That makes me smile.

From the lamps, I cannot but help notice the prayer hanging above my dresser. This prayer had also hung in my grandmother's bedroom. It had been my grandmother's favorite, according to my mother, and was read at her funeral. It is the prayer by Saint Francis of Assisi. I memorized this prayer recently and noticed, for the first time, how gentle I have become with myself. Every night I would stumble on the words, attempting to remember them. I love the rhythm of these words. This prayer has come to mean so much to me.

But I am not religious.

I have always considered myself to be spiritual in some type of "modern" sense. I have always believed that there is a God. Recently, little by little, my home has begun to reflect this—a deeper side, an inner side of my nature. I see this as I dust. I know when this began. I keep dusting. . . .

I enter my writing room with the dust rag and spray the antique desk with furniture polish. This desk once belonged to my other grandmother, the one who still lives close by. I feel a pang of guilt when I think of how I rushed to get her off the phone earlier, saying I had to clean. This is something I know she can appreciate. Cleaning. I rub the desk with polish. This desk had been with my grandmother ever since I can remember. When I was eight, I told her that someday if she wanted to give it away, I would "take it off her hands." That time came, and now this desk is in my home.

I take all the objects off the desktop. I look at the seashells I once gathered on a Florida beach. I see the picture of my stepdaughter holding her cat, Bob, in an old tarnished silver frame. I dust my favorite photo of our wedding. I then dust my antique perfume bottles. I rub the front of the desk. The wood seems so rich. I have never noticed it in this light before. I put an angel picture in a cubbyhole on one side of the desk. The cutout is in the shape of a crescent moon. My hand moves inside the moon, dusting.

I love the lines of this desk.

I move on to dust a small bookcase. As I did with the desk, I take everything off this bookcase and put it on the daybed we keep for company. I spray the top with polish.

It gleams. I first place a doily back on the top. This doily, I am sure, had also been my grandmother's. It was something she made, in between raising my father and working full time at a department store, in the women's clothing department. She had been a buyer and each year she had come from Austin, Minnesota, to the Twin Cities to buy clothes. My brother and sister and I always looked great after Grandma came to visit. We always got what didn't sell at the store. But it is this handmade gift, this piece of her, that means so much to me now.

Over time this bookcase has evolved into some type of sacred place for that and other objects that have meaning for me. My stepdaughter had given me a postcard of an Indian maiden. On the back, the card read, "She is innocence and all the colors will dance within her." I don't know why it resonated with me but it did. I place it back on the bookcase too. I replace the candlesticks from my old home. Wrapped around the top of one of them is a Rosary that my dear friend Margaret gave me last summer. I am not Catholic, but through a series of events, I have become interested in Rosaries. They seem exotic to me, full of mystery. Those Catholics have such wonderful rituals to fall back on: the incense and the waving of brass containers filled with smoke—all the stuff that makes you wonder. The beads are worn on this Rosary. This was particularly appealing, since a Catholic obviously had held them and used them. They were broken in. I just do not know how to use them.

Next, I place a pair of baby booties back on the doily. These booties belonged to my baby daughter, Grace. As I touch the soft fabric, my mind goes back to the days she was in the hospital, to her short five-week life. She died two years ago this month. I place a crystal on top of the booties, and I wonder if I will keep these booties here forever. Will there ever be a time that I will put them away?

This room had been her nursery, and now it is the room in which I write to her. I call it my writing room. I think of all that has happened in this room, of all the letters I have written to Grace here. I think of how I have cried so frequently in this room. I keep dusting.

I go over everything with my dust rag—my computer, the bedside table with a prayer book, the enameled frame of the daybed. Somehow, in doing this small chore, I am honoring Grace's memory and my life. Somehow, when I work like this, I honor who I was and who I have become. All these objects I touch as I dust are a part of me. They all mean something to me—to my past—and somehow they have propelled me to this moment. To this time, this exact space, of realization.

I realize that we lose something by not touching our things, by not bringing them out to look at. In the mere act of looking, we are taken back in time. All the feelings of that time surface like waves that break on a shoreline, only to flow back to some bigger body of water. Touch brings the glance, the memory, into a more physical reality. When I touch my daughter's baby booties, I can almost imagine touching her for that second. They are so soft, just as her skin had been.

I put my dust rag away.

Now as I sit here writing, I feel the breeze come through the curtain. I have paused here, in honor. By simply dusting, this sacredness has come about. As we rush through our days, speeding faster and faster to keep pace with it all, we lose something of ourselves. I know I have. I remember the pain and then the joy of knowing my daughter—of knowing myself. I think of the love and friendships that have sprung from her short life. I don't know why, but this makes me think of God. Was it the gratefulness of this moment?

Since Grace's life and death, God has kept popping up in the most unusual places for me. . . .

I.
LOSING

BEFORE

Hello Little One,   November 27, 1993

I want to let you know that I found out I was pregnant at my dear friend Deb's on November 2. I could not believe it. I was so surprised and happy. I drove home, and your father (for some reason) was out in front of the house waiting to let me in. It was a brisk evening. I ran up the steps, put my arms around him, and said, "We are going to have a baby!" I could tell he was as surprised as I was, and very pleased. He kept saying, "I don't believe it!" We were just beaming all evening and so excited. I called your Aunt Liz, my sister, and she made me tell my mother.

Your father kept trying to call your Grandma and Grandpa Love, but they were not home. Finally, we reached them, and they were as happy as we were. Today is two days past Thanksgiving, and there is beautiful snow on the ground. We put the Christmas tree up early so your sister, Amanda, could enjoy it longer. You are turning into a reality for me. I can feel that I love you already. I am so happy.

Dear One,   December 1993

Well, it's Sunday night. I have some beautiful medieval Christmas music on that your father really wanted me to play. Your sister is upstairs watching the *Flintstone's Christmas.* The house is warm and toasty as I write. The Christmas tree looks beautiful. I have felt a happiness lately that I have never felt before, and a connection to all things. Are you giving and producing those feelings within me?

Today your father and I went to a brunch for his work, and then we went to the Mall of America for Christmas shopping. We held hands and loved each other deeply. You are so lucky to have a father like him.

Let me tell you how I met your father. Twelve years ago I was interviewing for a job. Your father was standing in the office lobby as I walked through the doors for my interview. He offered me a cup of coffee. When I finished with the interview and went to the elevators to leave— there stood your father. I don't know why, but we ended up going out for lunch. And I didn't even know him!

That afternoon, he told me how he had just gotten back from Paris. He taught music there. When he came back to the United States, he found out his grandfather in Minneapolis had been very ill. So John, your father, came to the Twin Cities to care for him. Your great-grandfather eventually passed away, but your father stayed on in Minnesota.

Your father and I went out a couple of times back then. One night he made me this incredible lasagna dinner. It's funny what you remember when you look back, but this meal was perfect. It was the first meal a man had ever made for me. Your daddy played the saxophone for me that night. I could see how talented he was. Shortly after this, your father gave me a gift of a crystal heart to wear around my neck. He told me it was for courage in the future. I'll never forget that. . . .

Back then, your dad was very intense. He still is. He seemed like such an artist. He seemed so strong. As I look back now, I don't think I was ready for that type of intensity, not at first.

I went on to date and later marry another man. This marriage was very short-lived. Your father also had a brief marriage, in which his daughter Amanda was born. The odd thing about all of this was that our paths kept crossing every couple of years.

And then one day he called me at work, out of the blue. He said, "Hi, this is John Love." My heart melted. I have always loved his voice. It is so deep, so protective.

When we began dating in earnest, we were a threesome: your father, Amanda, and me.

I met Amanda before she could talk. She lived with your father part time, and so it became the three of us. When I made candlelight dinners during our courtship, it was always for three. It was when I saw your father with Amanda that I really began to love him. I saw how gentle he could be. I saw how much he loved his daughter, and it touched me deeply.

After dating for a while, your father took me to northern Minnesota under the pretense that we were going on a little getaway weekend. We arrived at this condominium on the shores of Lake Superior and he immediately wanted to take me hiking. I thought, *hiking?* But I went along with the idea reluctantly. What I didn't know was that your father wanted to ask me to marry him from one of the highest peaks in Minnesota.

I was sitting on a log, rubbing my feet in the middle of this forest when your father got down on his knees, right then and there, and proposed. I started crying and clinging to him. Your father said that I really deserved this—a total and complete proposal. . . .

We were married four months after this.

Hello little babe,   December 23, 1993

Last night we had an early Christmas at your Grandmother Sara's. Sara is my mother. We had dinner, opened presents from Liz, her husband, Dean, and Grandpa. Your sister, Amanda, got a new kitten named Bob, whom you will meet in July. She just loves him!

A week ago I was at the doctor's and heard your heartbeat. It was so strong. It made you feel like a true reality. I got tears in my eyes. Daddy and I will be celebrating our first Christmas Eve in this house. We love you.

Dear baby,   December 1993

I am so happy. Christmas is close, and I am in the middle of buying presents. I keep wrapping things and putting them under the tree. Daddy and I are going to be having my friend Julie, whom I work with at the university, and her husband, Kelly, over tonight. The best part of this is that Julie is pregnant too! Although we are nine years apart in age—I'm the older one—it feels wonderful to be able to share this experience with another woman. Julie and I compare notes, about morning sickness and what tastes good. Her baby is due right after you are. Only three days apart! Can you imagine? I tease Julie that if I have a boy—which I think you are—and if she has a girl, we could hook you two up when you're older! I get such a kick out of that—imagining you as some wonderful little boy running around, making your father and me laugh!

Dear Peanut,   January 16, 1994

We call you Peanut because a while ago, I tried to explain to your sister, Amanda, how big you were, and *peanut* was the only word that worked. So, hello little Peanut.

Right now, I am sitting in front of the fire, writing and listening to classical music. It is Sunday morning and the snow is falling outside. The weather has been so cold it makes you cry.

Your father is upstairs reading the paper and probably watching TV. I like the calm peacefulness after a long week at work. I saw your Aunt Liz and cousin Sarah yesterday. Sarah is growing so much. She is a sweetheart.

I have felt some movement and flutterings. I could not believe it. You seem to move when I am resting. I wonder what you are doing downstairs! Until the next time I write, dear one. I love you so much.

Dear Baby,   January 17, 1994
(a letter from your sister, Amanda)

Mom said that it was vary hard to have a baby. I'm looking forward to seeing you at age eight. I want to teach you how to talk, and read, and everything like that. I LOVE YOU.   SINSIRELY, ∾ Amanda Love
P.S. I will help you with your homework.

Dear One,   January 17, 1994

Today, your father and I went to the doctor's and had a picture taken of you. You are so cute. You moved your legs and arms and turned around in my stomach. Your heart was going like mad. We both feel you are so much alive. We love you so much! You are coming around July 9. The nurse thought this was right. I called Grandma Sara and Aunt Liz and told them.

Little Peanut,   February 15, 1994

I was at the doctor's and heard your heartbeat again. I
wish I could find out if you are a girl or a boy. It is in your
chart, but I promised Dad that I would not really find out.
I told them at the clinic not to let me know. Anyway, it is
very difficult because the information is there. No problem though; either way, you will be loved. We love you
now! I do wish that I could see you and say hello.

Dearest One,   March 28, 1994

Well, it has been a long time since I have written. Much
has been going on. Your father and I finished your room
last weekend. It took much longer than we had thought.
But we got your crib up and moved the TV room downstairs. Dad is now working in the basement, getting the
French doors ready for the new TV room. It is all very
nice.

You have been kicking and rolling and turning like
crazy. You really enjoy being up at night. Almost every
night I get up because you like to move or I have to go to
the bathroom. I can tell you must be getting bigger
because my appetite is getting stronger. I go into the nursery and look at your bed and I think that you will be in it
soon. It is such a sweet room. Right close to Dad and me.

Amanda, your sister, is at my mother's now for school
break. She is playing with my brother's daughter, your
cousin Emily. Emily, Aunt Betsy, and my brother Charlie
(your uncle) will be reunited in Washington, DC, where

they have moved and bought a house. Uncle Charlie got a new job. Your Aunt Betsy wanted to finish her degree here at the university before joining him, and they did not want to have Emily switch school in the middle of the year. I wish that they did not have to move, but that is life.

Dearest child, April 1994

I just wanted to let you know, my little baby, that you are precious to me. I feel you inside of me. So active and growing and strong. Already, you have a mind of your own. I play a game with you. I think of you and, to see if you are thinking of me, I wait for you to move and you do! There is a bond between us that even you can feel.

You have taught me so many things in such a short time. I quit smoking because I wanted your lungs to be clean. I am watching my diet so you have the right nutrients. All of this started out just for you, but it has also influenced me as to how I live my life. I want to thank you for your wisdom at such a young age. You are amazing!

You seem to like the evening hours, another trait I understand. I do my best thinking at 3 A.M The house is quiet and we have it all to ourselves as we prowl downstairs to read, to watch TV, or to simply just be who we are. No interruptions, right?

How can I tell you that having you in my life, right now, has made me a better person? That giving to you before you are born is a side of me that I never knew I had. That protecting you from harm and being your champion are things I had heard about from others, but that I felt were depths unreachable to me.

I ask myself, as I scurry through my busy days, how can all of this be happening to me? How can you penetrate through my most controlling habits and let me know that now it is time to rest, and now it is time to be active, and most of all that some things just have to wait?

Somehow you knew. You appeared in my life at just the right time, to teach me just the right things.

Darling baby,   May 1994

Tonight your father and I sat out on the back porch, the little one on the second floor. I guess people used to call them "shaker porches" because they would shake their rugs out on them. Dad and I sit out there after work and watch the clouds go by. The evenings are so beautiful. I wear an old robe and pull my hair back. Dad shows me the clouds. Honey, I think that you are bringing your father and me closer. Tonight Daddy took a picture of me with these funny glasses on. Then he wanted one of my stomach. I let him do it because it makes him happy. It is so funny, but sometimes he watches me take a bath. He sits on the floor and looks at my body. I feel so big, but he loves this miracle as much as I do. I feel this from him. He is so proud of both you and me.

We talk and talk out on that porch. I have never noticed clouds like I have recently. You and Daddy are showing me so much.

Dearest child,   June 12, 1994

Today I went to the clinic to have an ultrasound done, because I am gestationally diabetic and the doctors wanted to know your position. I was lying in a dark room while the technician did the procedure. Suddenly she went outside for a moment, and I started feeling scared. She came back with a doctor, who then went over my stomach again with this instrument. There was so much silence in the room, and I felt one tear roll down my cheek in the dark. The doctor went over my stomach again and, again. He said things like, "Did you see the head?" and, "The heart is enlarged." The doctor then turned on the lights and told me that something was very wrong. He wanted me to see a specialist. The doctor put me in a room with Kleenex and a telephone, so I could call family members. I was so alone.

I tried to call your father but could not get through. I called Margaret, another friend I work with at the university, and I could not hold my tears back. I started crying so hard—I don't know what I told her. I remember her saying "Yes, yes, yes," like she understood. I told her how I was alone in a room with Kleenex. I felt her alarm—just like mine—I felt it through the telephone wire.

My dearest child,   June 1994

As I told you, last week I had an ultrasound during a routine checkup, and the doctor performing the ultrasound said your heart and brain looked somewhat enlarged. After I went into a panic, Grandma Sara came to be with me in the waiting room, at a clinic for pediatric specialists. Your father left work to be with me. When Grandma and I saw him come through the clinic doors, we both somehow relaxed. I was so happy to see him. I was so grateful that Grandma could even sit and wait with me. We found out that things were not as bad as first portrayed.

Tonight, Dad and I were talking about you on the back porch, and we know you will be unique and strong and beautiful. I feel you move and I am so happy. Please know how much we love you and how much you have entered our lives and changed them for the better.

Dearest child,   June 1994

Last night I had a dream that scared me. I told your Aunt Liz about it when she called. I think she became upset with me. I have to write this.

I saw the face of a child—it was almost transparent and it had a golden hue to it. The face kept fading and fading until it was gone, like the still pictures of a camera. The baby was fair and its eyes looked at me. In the next scene of the dream, I saw another child's face—this time in full color, not the faded golden color of the first child. This new child's hair was dark like your father's. I knew when I awoke that something was wrong, very wrong, with the first child. That is the feeling I had. The second face was strong and healthy. I feel unnerved by this. I am now thinking maybe I will have a girl and not a boy as I had once thought. Maybe that is what this dream means.

I will write later.

Dear child,   June 1994

It has been hard for me the last two weeks. Dr. Calvin, a pediatric specialist, told me that you could possibly have a heart problem. I have been up night after night wondering what all this means, most of all to you and then to me. It has been one of the most painful experiences that I have ever undergone. Then I feel you move and I know how strong you really are. No one can ever really understand this feeling unless they have gone through the process of fear and hope. You are the sweetest of things, and I am so excited that you will be here soon. I packed our bags for the hospital.

Dear little baby,   July 1994

There has been much that has happened in the last week. Dr. Calvin told us that you may have a heart condition. I have worried so much, but I have faith in the specialists that will be close by to help. We are scheduled to be at a different hospital that specializes in these issues.

I feel you move around, and you seem to be getting ready to be born. You move at the darndest times. Usually at night. I have been up at night thinking many times. It has given me the quiet time I need. I see many beautiful things like the moon and the rising sun, and I hear all the chirping birds. This calms me in so many ways. It will be soon that we meet. I love all that you are.

July 3, 1994

I am waiting for you to be born. Your father and I have spent the weekend on hold. I could tell that your father wanted to go agate hunting but would not leave me alone in case you decided to come. I have stopped working so I can get the rest I need and also to make sure your heart will be strong enough. I have been sleeping quite a bit recently. This is all different for me because I am used to being more active, but I guess I need the rest.

I had a bad night last night. I could not sleep. I kept getting up and going downstairs. I cried, thinking that I might have done something to have caused you these problems. I keep trying to think what it was. Was I sick, and you got what I had? Maybe I didn't eat enough vegetables. Maybe it was the coffee I drank sometimes. What was it and how has it affected you? I keep worrying and wondering what it could be. I have all these thoughts in my mind. I wonder what you feel and if you can feel what I feel. I keep thinking that if you can, you may not be getting enough strength from me. I worry that, because I am worried, you will have doubts about your place in this life, and I do not mean for you to feel like that at all. I feel so bad when I have feelings of doubt, because you are not getting the positive energy that you should have from me. I have to say these things because they are true. They are a part of me—a part that I am not proud of. But please realize that this is my fear, not yours.

You will soon be independent when you are born, and I will be able to take care of you and see how you respond. It is so difficult when I am just waiting. Your father does not know what to do with me at this point. I know that he has his feelings, but he does not want to worry me. Well, I must go. Bye-bye.

GRACIE'S LIFE

My darling daughter,

You were born on July 22, 1994, at 10:30 A.M. I had been in labor for two and a half days. It was tough going then, but I knew I would see you soon, so that kept me going. I felt so close to you then. With each contraction, we were together. I could not wait to see you. Your father was there every step of the way. He stayed at the hospital with me, sleeping in a chair.

The doctors put me on potosin to go into labor because it was ten days past my due date. Each contraction was like a wave. There was some pain and then it subsided. I basically felt like I was in a different world. The only thing that kept me focused was the thought of you.

My water broke on Thursday sometime, yet my cervix never opened. By Thursday night, the doctor planned on a cesarean and I knew you would come the next day. I was calm. I knew we would be together. Your father was wonderful. He was in the operating room. You will see how soothing he is. He sat by my side and later told me he had looked into the area you came out of. He said that the space was huge. The doctor had to bat my uterus around to get it back in shape before he could put it back in my body.

After I woke up from the surgery, I was rushed to my new room, put on my bed, and then wheeled through a tunnel, which was a city-block long, to see you. I was under morphine for pain by this time. When I laid eyes on you, I thought God had given me the most wonderful, unique angel I had ever seen. You were so beautiful and perfect. You were incredible. I started crying—everyone did. I loved you completely when we met. The nurse asked what your name was. Your name, which your father actually picked out, became Grace Zuri Love. Dad was reading *The New Yorker* one night out on the porch, and he said, "What about Grace?" I loved it immediately. We were then reading in a book of names and came across the name Zuri. It meant "beautiful" in Swahili. I loved the sound phonetically; so did your father. It all came together when we saw your little face. I have to pause and cry at times because so much of this is hard to write.

When I saw you for the first time, I knew that you were my angel. Oh darling girl, I love you so. We all were admiring your beauty, because when I saw you, I knew that for the first time in my life, I knew true love. I have never felt this, ever. There you were, and I was crying with so much happiness—I was overwhelmed. A doctor had been writing in a chart across the room; he raced over and told all of us, your Aunt Liz, Daddy, and me, that this was not a time to be happy. That your condition was very serious. I knew something was wrong because you had a breathing tube in, but I did not know what. . . .

I had been so happy and then my tears turned to fear, Grace. Please forgive me. I want to be strong for you.

Later that day, we were told by a Dr. Meyer that there was an arterial/ventricle malformation in your head. The arterial/ventricle malformation is a malformation of a vein. It can happen anywhere on the body, and surgery can usually correct it. Yet because of the location of this in your head, it is difficult to correct. Although this malformation is simply in the veins near the outside of your head, it has affected the main vein in your neck and is pumping blood rapidly to your heart. This vein has enlarged due to this and, consequently, it has enlarged your heart. It is like a river going into your heart. The surgeons are attempting to stop this blood flow, but the surgeries have to be done in your head. Your veins are so tiny, they keep collapsing.

When I got the news about how bad the malformation was, I started crying. All of this is so hard, and you are so tiny. Otherwise, you are perfect.

Grandma Sara stayed at the hospital with me at night, to keep me company. I kept working on getting stronger to see you. That is all I thought about. By Monday, an emergency surgery had to be performed—your heart would have given out, it was beating so fast.

Gracie,   July 1994

I am still at the hospital. I am trying so hard to regain my strength so I can be there for you. I know I already mentioned that my mother stays at the hospital with me at night. Daddy is watching Amanda at home. I think the hospital is making him nervous. Grandma walked with me tonight around the nurses' station. It is the first time I have walked that much and it was difficult, but I just focus on how much you will need me. I have to be strong for you. I am so grateful for your grandmother, Gracie. I know this is hard for her, but I am optimistic. I showed a nurse your picture tonight. I said, "Do you want to see my daughter?" It was the first time I ever called you my daughter. Grandma turned her head from me. I think she may have started crying. I am so proud of you. I have to keep thinking positively so you can get better, Darling.

Today Daddy took me to see you. He wheeled me in a wheelchair all the way to the intensive care unit. We were at an elevator somewhere in the hospital when Daddy kneeled down by my feet, took my hand, and said that we would always be together, no matter what happened. He just looked at me with such big eyes when he said that. He is so gentle. But I wonder if he knows something I do not. I am going to get strong, Grace. I know that if I think good things, then maybe you will be fine. I know your condition is severe, but I am so strong as a person. I have always been able to get through tough times somehow. We will get through this, Grace. I promise.

I am tired, honey.

Darling Girl,   July 1994

Today Dad and I were in the intensive care unit watching you. We just watch you and are full of wonder. You are to have your second surgery. I get so worried when this happens. Each time, Dad just paces. I am still in the wheelchair. Then a nurse asked us if we wanted a chaplain. *A chaplain?* I thought. *Why?*

And then I realized what she was saying. I can hardly write these words.

A man, the chaplain, came to us soon after this. His name was Okon. He was from Nigeria and is a Presbyterian, which is what I am. He held a shell with water in it and said some words as he baptized you. I was crying so hard I had to hold on to your little bed in order to stand; I could not see you if I sat in that wheelchair. A nurse started crying too. We all were crying. No one had told me you could die.

27

Gracie, July 1994

Today I watched your father with you at your bedside. I watched his face. I watched how he talked to the nurse, asking about your breathing and heartbeat. I saw him as so beautiful—his quiet way of expression, his calming effect on people—especially me. He caught my eye, and we both looked at you. And never have I seen a more beautiful child. I know Dad felt it too. We touched your little toes.

Dearest Grace, July 1994

Margaret stopped by our home a couple days ago with a book for me, *Care of the Soul,* by Thomas Moore. We both love books—we both love words so much. She just looked so normal.

She asked about you. I wanted to tell her so much more than I did. Gracie, I know she wants to help. I just know she does. . . .

But I can't let anyone in now. I think I have used all my feelings up.

Dear Daughter, August 1994

I felt so guilty yesterday. Everyone at the hospital has told both Dad and me that we need to take some time off—away from the hospital. Dad does this every now and then, but I have only missed seeing you one day. That was the day after my cesarean.

Yesterday I went to get a haircut. Judy, who cuts Dad's

hair, asked about you. She gave me a card with the patron saint Jude on it. I am not Catholic, but I will take anything now—everything, if it will help you. Judy told me that miracles happen. I believe that too. You have made it through so many surgeries. I keep hoping. . . .

Grace, I know this is crazy, but I try to look pretty for you. I comb my hair and put on lipstick, in hopes that you see your mother as beautiful, as I see you. I try to be optimistic. But it is getting harder. A fear has come into my life that I have never known. I cry and cry. The other night when Dad and I were out on the porch, he told me that I would have made a good mother. I was furious. I am a mother now! Doesn't he see that? Gracie, I felt so much anger when he said that! He has Amanda. He can watch her grow and run and play! Doesn't he know that is all I want?

When he said that, I wanted to run and leave him and Amanda. I want this pain to leave. I want to be able to have my life the way it was, with you in it. I cannot even tell him how much this pain hurts.

Dad got up and left me on the porch alone after this. I just gripped the railing and wondered, *How will this end? How can I survive?* I went back inside the house. I knew then, I could not leave you alone in this world.

Grace,   August 1994

I am here again writing because I just need to express what is going on. There is so much happening so fast. I feel as if I am mechanical, going through motions. Dad and I never eat during the day. We only eat at night. We drink coffee during the day—all day at the hospital. We have discovered a place outside of the intensive care unit where we can go to get away from things, in the sun. It is there that we talk about all that the doctors have said. We discuss every detail of your condition. But it is the sun that I love, when we sit there with our coffee cups. It is by the children's play area, which is for the siblings of children who are sick in the hospital. Sometimes your Grandma Sara joins us and we talk. My sister, Liz, has left her family so often to be here also.

Deb Kelley, my dear friend, has organized dinners to be brought to us each night. She has called all my friends and everyone has a night to fix us dinner. I can't believe anyone would think of that.

Deb Bohnen, my best friend, has become some type of central station. I call her almost every day to tell her the news. She then passes this on to whoever needs to know. I just cannot be on the phone. I cannot talk to people now. I have gone so far inward. The other night your father was late, and I went into a panic thinking he might have driven off the road or was in some type of car accident. I called Deb and left her a message. She came over at 11 P.M. to be with me. We just sat and talked, and I cried. Oh, Gracie. . . .

I ask myself, *How can there be this much love in the world? How can these people come, almost out of the woodwork, to help us?* It seems as if strangers are extending their love to us somehow. We meet other parents in the intensive care unit, and we are bonded together by the love of our children. Gracie, all the medical staff shows you, and us, so much love. But they do not even know us.

Darling Gracie,   August 16, 1994

I spoke to Sandy, your night nurse, at 6:30 A.M. She said you had slept on your stomach. You need to rest to get your strength up. I will be going into the hospital soon. I am bringing some shirts Grandma Sara got you and booties and a mobile. Your blood pressure is down a little and you are voiding. Yesterday, you had your eyes open and you were trying to focus. When you look at me, you give me the world. I adore you.

I have to keep in mind that those tubes are saving your life. I worry so much that you may be in pain, darling. The thought constantly makes me cry and my throat hurts. You are incredibly brave and strong. You give me strength.

Daddy goes to see you after work, and I am there during the day. We love you so much, sweetheart. Thank you for blessing our lives. I love you, darling.

Dearest child,   August 1994

I am at the hospital now. We did your hair and put a shirt on you. Karen, one of your nurses, said I could hold you. I can't believe it. I only could hold you one other

31

time, and you are nearly a month old. You look so sweet. You are so courageous. Your little eyes are wide open. I brought your mobile in today so you can focus a little bit. The doctor wants you back on your feedings again today. Your little digestive track is slow because of your medication. Your blood pressure is good, in the 70s and 80s. Your heart rate is in the 140s. You are also going to the bathroom on your own. I have your wonderful baby smell on my hands. The weather is turning fall-like. I will be going back to work on Monday. I need to start getting ready for that. I am going back in to see you now, sweetie pie.

Darling Grace,   August 1994

One of the internists, a woman, came to do rounds on you. I was feeling so good to be there, next to you. She checked you while I held you, and she told me that things are not good. I said, "You mean she may not survive?" When she nodded, I sat and held you and tears came down my cheeks. She was so gentle, as gentle as anyone could be. I tried to contain myself, but there is no way that I will ever understand this pain. I have no words left.

Gracie,   August 18, 1994

I am in a coffee shop now, having some coffee. I had a bad day yesterday. I thought I saw a tear in your eye and I thought you were in pain, and my heart tore in half. The thought of you being in any pain makes me crazy. I look at your beautiful eyes and I want to give you the world. I keep thinking that when you look at me, you think, "Why Mom, why?" Yet you are so brave. Those tubes and everything bother me so much sometimes, sweetheart. You mean the world to me. Every day I cry for you. If I could only take your place. If I could only lie beside you and keep you in my arms all night. Gracie, when I write these words, I cry, darling. I am on the way to the hospital now. I paid bills earlier. I must buy stamps. I tried to pick things up a little. The house has been kind of disorganized. I still cannot find my work clothes. I am going from maternity clothes to regular, from summer to fall.

I look at your room and I think maybe I will see you in it! I imagine you in your crib with no tubes. You are a miracle. I love your curly hair, just like Daddy's. Your forehead and eyebrows are Daddy's also. I think you may have my lips and coloring.

Will you forgive me for not being able to stay twenty-four hours a day at the hospital? I stay as long as I can. And next week I have to go back to work.

Sandy, your nurse, will be on nights again soon. She is so good with you. She really knows how to do your hair. Our nickname for you (really it's mine) is Gracie Boo. Daddy calls you the "Eveready Bunny," like the bunny in those battery commercials.

When I write this, it is as if I am talking to you. Even as I carried you, we had a connection, especially at night. You would move like crazy. It always made me feel secure to know you were alive. Your alertness at night is so much like me. I'm always thinking and problem solving at night, and somehow I always have the energy and answers the next day.

Darling girl, hang in there, keep living, and know that Daddy and I love you more than the stars in the sky. You can do this, Gracie Boo. Mama is on her way to the hospital. With love, hopes, and dreams. . . .

Darling Gracie,   August 21, 1994
Tomorrow you will be one month old. I cannot believe it. I love you so.

Today, when I saw you, it seemed as if you could focus a little better. Your eyes have been moving around quite a bit, and you quiver sometimes, possibly due to your drug withdrawal, as the doctors decrease your medication. I spoke to a neurologist today, and they will be giving you some tests this week. They feel you may have some neurological damage. I see you and I see a lovely, courageous child who so would love to live. I see your little face and that circular little mouth you make when you get a little shaky. Oh, darling, I want you to be safe and strong. Daddy and I have tried to save your life through the surgeries seven times. If we hadn't tried all these things, you would not be alive today. I hope you can feel and know this. Please try and be brave and know that God is with you, that the doctors are helping you, and that Daddy and I will never leave you.

Sweetie Pie, August 22, 1994

I am waiting at the bus stop to ride to my office. I spoke to Sandy, your night nurse, and she said you had a fun night last night. You had a bath. You kicked your legs and also tried to focus more with your eyes. Sandy is so good for you.

It is my first day back to work. I think about how you and I waited at these bus stops when I was pregnant with you. It was you and me. Me and my baby.

You are starting to breathe on your own. There possibly may be a little neurological damage from your surgeries and the malformation. We can cross that bridge when we come to it. Your eyes seem to be able to open a little wider. I believe in you so much. You are one month old today! Happy Birthday!

Darling daughter, August 23, 1994

I stopped by the hospital before work started today. You were sleeping. You were not up a lot last night. Today you go for a CT scan. They are checking your brain to see how it is working. Your respiratory machine was turned down to twelve breaths per minute, but your CO_2 level went up. I worry about your breathing, your pain, and at times your sleeping. You are my angel, that is why.

Today you looked so peaceful, so beautiful. Your lips are gorgeous. Your hair is light brown, almost blond, and curly. Your skin is so smooth. I look at you and cannot help but be captivated by your beauty. Your hands and fingers are so perfectly shaped. I want to hurry you home, take care of you, protect you, love you with all my heart, darling. I'm at the bus stop again. It looks like rain today.

I have a confession to make. I smoked ten cigarettes after I spoke to a doctor last week. I could not stand the pain any longer, and so I weakened. I have not touched one since then. Your father was furious with me. We fought for two days before we resolved the conflict. It is so hard for both Mom and Dad at times, honey. We love you so much and cannot think of anything else.

Sweetheart,   August 1994
Daddy called at work today and said you have water in the ventricles in your head. The doctors need to perform another surgery at 6 P.M. tonight. I am waiting at the bus stop again to catch a ride to our car. Everyone at work asked about you today. I feel so upset that you have to go through another surgery, honey. It is too much for anyone. When will this end? Why has this happened? You are so innocent. I don't want you to suffer, darling. Please know Mama loves you and that I will be by you no matter what transpires. I am going to the hospital now so I can hold you. You are my angel. I love you so.

Darling child,   August 1994
Daddy and I have been talking about you every night and every moment of the day. Your father and I haven't left each other's sides for days, when we are at the hospital

or at home. The doctors said there was nothing more they could do for you. We, in turn, came to the decision that your life is in God's hands. God help us all.

Grace Darling,   August 28, 1994

Today we are in a private room with you. It seems as though the end may be near. Dad and I are with you. Okon, the chaplain, came to be with us. He had the day off, but he heard that you may be dying, so he came. People keep appearing out of nowhere. Okon sang "Jesus Loves Me" with his sweet accent. Grace, I have turned to stone. I feel myself hardening against life. How can this be real? Where did God go?

Why can't it be me instead of you?

AFTER

Dearest Daughter,   September 1, 1994

  You left this earth on August 29, 1994. I write here at five
in the morning. I am sitting outside, waiting for the sun
to come up. I hear the birds, and the paper woman just
dropped off the paper. I told her you had died. She looked
at me silently—not saying anything, probably wondering
how this woman could be sitting here, practically in the
dark, smoking a cigarette. I have my journal with me—I
am going to read a passage of it for your service. Grace, I
am in a place where nothing touches me. I feel so
wooden. I go through motions, but it is as if I am looking

38

at myself from the outside. I have left who I was.

Gracie, here comes the sun with all its streaks of pink in the sky. Where are you?

Dear Grace,   September 1994

We had your service and it was beautiful. There were so many people there. I kept looking for Julie, my good friend from work, but couldn't see her. Finally, at the lunch at our house, someone told me that she was out of town. I miss her so much. No one had told me she would be gone.

Dearest Child,   September 1994

For some reason, I can't stop thinking about the day you died. Daddy was holding you in his arms—he and Grandpa were sitting with you in the private room. You had your little fingers wrapped around Daddy's thumb. Then you died—you were just gone.

But Gracie, I was not there. I was in another room lying down. Dad made me go lie down, because he thought we would be at the hospital for a long time. And then you were gone. Just gone. I held you and rocked you after you died . . . but I had no idea, not one inkling how much I would miss you. I felt like stone—like I had turned to stone.

You died with Daddy. Grace, you didn't wait for me. Everyone made me lie down. I didn't want to. And then you were gone.

Have I done something wrong? Will you ever forgive me, darling daughter, for not being there? Gracie, my heart is breaking. . . .

Dearest Daughter,   September 1994

I just remembered a day when you were still alive. Daddy and I had come back from the hospital. I was outside sitting on the back steps, waiting for your father to join me. I heard these funny noises coming from the house. I could not place the noise at all, so I went inside. There was your father on the floor of the sunroom. He was all alone; his head was in his hands. It was his sobs that I heard. My heart broke with the sound. I went to put my arms around him, and he looked at me. He promised me we would always be a family, no matter what happened. That's just what he said, Grace, "You, and I, and Gracie will always be a family." I know he meant Amanda too.

Grace,   September 1994

Some time has passed since you left us. I keep reflecting on things. I have to tell you about something that happened the day we were planning your service with Okon. When we got home from the hospital, my eyes flew to the dining-room table, which was covered with pictures of you. Madeline, my friend Margaret's mother, had brought us some flowers and they were way at one end of the table. My favorite picture of you was at the other end, and my eyes went right to it. There were three little stems of baby's breath surrounding your little face in a perfect circle. I knew that these represented you, me, and Daddy. I knew that you were trying to tell me that all was okay. You were fine. Gracie, I told your father and he just stared at me. But I know this is so. I know it is. I keep thinking of those little flowers, on my favorite picture.

Dearest Gracie,   September 1994

Today I saw Julie. She is on maternity leave with her son, Peter, but today she came in to work. I heard someone say, "Julie is here." My heart started beating hard. She came into our office and asked to see me in the hallway. It was the only place we could be alone. I went out with her and we just stood there facing each other. She started saying, "I am sorry. I am so sorry," over and over and over. She gave me a pin, an angel pin. We both started crying and I saw her eyes and I cried harder. I look at her eyes, Grace, and I know she feels my pain. And all I want is just who she is—Julie. That is all I want. I have missed her so much. I don't know why, but I see my heart in her eyes. . . .

Darling Daughter,   October 17, 1994

You are in heaven now. I cannot believe that you are not here. This past weekend we took down your crib. It was so sad. Daddy unscrewed all the bolts and nuts, and I looked at him. We both felt that we would never have to do this. We put up a daybed in your room—which has really turned into my room. Last night I lay in there and just cried. I could not believe you were really not going to come home. I guess that by keeping your things around, I kept you alive on a certain level. You are my angel. I still love you with all my heart. Can you feel it in the clouds above?

My throat aches for you now. As I write this, tears come down my cheeks. Daddy got me a CD player for our new room. I can play music now. It really is quite nice. But it is only an object. It is not you. I think your father feels so bad. He had a rock engraved for you with your name on it for our wildflower garden. I think Dad really wants to make things up to me, as if I can't be happy now that you are gone. He is such a good man. But doesn't he know that no thing can take your place?

Last week, I really wished that I could hold you one more time. I really had a hard time with that, I didn't hold you enough when you were alive. Oh, darling child.

Until we talk again.

Gracie,   October 1994

I felt so low today. Tonight, I am up, wandering around the house. Everyone is asleep but me. It seems as if all the world is quiet, but inside I am torn to pieces. I got out your picture—the one that was in your service, the one with me touching your face. I started crying again. I kissed the glass of the picture, and it was so cold. Gracie, why did you leave me?

Dearest Grace,   October 1994

I am distant from your father now. It is as if we both have our ways of dealing with your death. I still want to cry, and your father wants to move on. He told me today that you were dead. Like I didn't know that! I think he does not want to hear me talk about you. He wants life to go on. We try to talk and end up fighting. It is because of this, Gracie, that I turn to this writing as my solace, that I sit down at my computer in your old room. It is all that I have, it seems.

Almost every night I cry. While your dad sleeps, I cry. Some type of fear has taken hold of me. If death can happen to a baby like you, what does that say about life? I know that I do not fear for my safety—Gracie, I don't know what to do.

Dear Grace,   October 1994

The funniest thing has been occurring recently. This started after you died. At night, it feels as if the down comforter on our bed is being tucked around me from the inside out. It is as if there is an exact outline of my body being made. I keep looking in the dark when this happens. But it is so consoling. You know that I always think of you when this happens. I think of you now, when anything happens—like when my computer screen glows. I've noticed it seeming to glow at night, Gracie, after I write to you, but when I get up to turn it off, I find it was never on. Grace, I think that if you can

43

connect to me, then maybe this is you or something. And then I fall asleep just thinking of you.

Darling Grace,   October 1994

I have been in Boston for work. Margaret and I go to these conventions every year. We work for a health care program at the university, and we promote the program at these conventions. I talked quite a bit to Margaret about you. She listens so well. The nice thing about her and me is that we are both the same age, we both love to read, and we are both usually in bed with a book by 7 P.M.!

Anyway, when I was getting dressed one morning for the convention, I looked in the mirror and saw my face, and for some reason, I thought of how you looked so much like Daddy. When I looked at my eyes, it seemed as if your eyes were like mine at that moment, and it almost felt as if you were looking through my eyes. This was only momentary, but the feeling was strong.

That night, after Margaret turned off her reading light, I continued to read. Finally, I turned off my light and went to sleep. I was awakened about 1 A.M. by a child's voice saying, "Mommy, Mommy." For a split second, I thought it might have been Amanda, that I was at home. But then I realized I was in Boston. I looked at the window and saw that the drapes were partially open. A little cloud floated by. I fell asleep, once again thinking of you. But that voice, Grace, was such a tiny, tinkly, far-off voice. Was that you?

When I later told Julie about this, she said that clouds don't float that low. I had never thought of that.

Hello little one,   November 2, 1994

Isn't it ironic? This is the exact day a year ago that I found out I was pregnant with you. I was so happy and excited. I was so filled with wonder. At last you were going to be in my life. I had waited so long to have you. I wanted you to have the right daddy. And then there he was, and you were to be in my life, and everything was going to be wonderful.

But Grace, that isn't happening. You died and my dreams crashed like glass around me. Now your father and I are not talking. He thinks he doesn't have any say with me, that I always get my way. When I open my mouth to say anything, he gets mad and walks away. Amanda is acting out in school. What's left? Everything is going haywire. I do not know how I can keep it together. I miss you so much. I drive home every night and cry. Tears come to my eyes on the bus. I find that I have gotten shy and quiet. I have never been at a loss for words, but now I am. I used to see the good in things, but now I feel empty. I thought, the other day, that I do not have a purpose. What am I going to do? What Gracie? What?

Some women are born to sorrow. I read that in a book once. Maybe I am one of those women. All I can think of is, where is my baby? Why can't I see you? I pray that you will show yourself to me somehow. There is all this talk about angels now. I read where people have actually seen angels. I guess that God does not want me to see you. Maybe this is some karmic debt I have to pay off, some lesson I have to learn. Life can be cruel. I know that people have lost loved ones before, but I never believed it could happen to me.

I have cried and cried as I wrote this. Amanda tried to come into the writing room (your nursery), and I told her I was busy. When I left to get toilet paper to wipe my eyes, she called out, "Mom." I dried my eyes quickly and went to see what she wanted. We read stories—some fables—together. She asked if I had been crying. I told her yes, and then she wanted to know if that was why I would not let her in the room. I told her yes, and she said that it was okay.

Somehow I feel more normal after reading those stories. Your father still is not really talking to me except for business matters. What does he want from me? He thinks I do not hear a word he says, but I hear everything. He won't hear me. He does not realize how strong he is. He wants to influence and influence. It really gets my dander up, but you know there is no one whom I respect more. My heart hurts when we are at these impasses. Things should be so much easier than this, but you know that sometimes the simple things are the hardest. Should I go and try to talk to him again? Oh, sweetheart, it feels as if I am talking to you in some way. Like this computer is our connection.

I don't know if you remember this, but after one of

your surgeries, you were so quiet and still and beautiful. I reached out to touch your face, and my hand was shaking really badly. There was such a big lump in my throat. I swallowed my tears and tried to be brave. I kept thinking that if I was strong, somehow you would sense this and get strength from me. But I could not hold you then. You had to lie in that bed all by yourself, so alone. Gracie, will you ever forgive me for not holding you enough? I didn't know that time would run out. And now there is no more time. All I have now to be close to you are these computer keys. Writing is the only action I can take. And the fact of the matter is, I would give anything to touch you again. Just your little hand or your little toes.

I better close now, but I just hate to say good-bye.

Grace,   November 3, 1994

Things have gone from bad to worse. I just spoke to your father. He thinks I control too many things, and that he cannot be different from me. That somehow I force my will on him. He said that he feels humiliated by me when I do this. He feels that everything is on my terms. I stood there and just cried. I have so much to go through now, as I am sure he does, and yet he does not tell me these things as they are happening. I find out this way. He must have built these things up inside. He said he needs space. That things just have to be left to be.

As he told me these things, I felt his pain. I did hear him. I asked him if this had just happened, or was it the way I was? He said he didn't know. I tried to hug him, and I bumped his glasses—another thing that drives him up the wall. I felt like such an idiot. I wanted to tell him about the pain I felt with your death and how hard it has gotten for me recently. But I couldn't. His expression seemed to be more important at the time.

I am worried. I feel that he needs time, and I need to express and make things come forth through communication. I make him nervous and he drives me crazy by not wanting to talk. Then I feel controlled. Then the cycle starts. This is very difficult. It is so painful. We are at such a delicate time in our relationship. We are only two years into our marriage, Amanda is having attention problems at school, and you have died—it has all combined into this boundaryless mass that leaks into all areas. We search and each come up with our own conclusions, so sure that the other will understand as we present our cases, not realizing that the other does not have the patience or the strength to be receptive to new ideas. It is such a luxury, really, to hear someone for what they are, and in a time of crisis, it is almost impossible.

I'm running out of steam. For the first time in our marriage, I am really frightened. It feels as if we could lose this, like our relationship is really threatened right now.

Darling Daughter,   November 4, 1994

How is heaven, sweet angel? It is Friday and things are quieter than they were earlier this week. Amanda is at her mother's house, and your father is downstairs reading. He still does not really want to deal with me, so I am left with all my feelings. You are my only solace. I look forward to talking to you this way. It is as if we have our own special time.

I saw Deb Bohnen this evening, and I talked to her about you. She talked about her life. Somehow, no matter what Deb and I are going through, when we get together, we end up feeling better.

And yet, I feel lonely tonight. Daddy is not ready to open up. He is having problems inside himself. I know he wants to practice his music, I know he would love to record songs, but he has not even played CDs since you died. So now there is no music in his life. It makes me so sad. Maybe he has just not had the time he needs to play. But I too feel as if I am put on hold, with no way for resolution.

Darling Daughter,   November 14, 1994

Tonight things look better than they have in a long time. This past weekend, we started to be a family again. Amanda and I went to a movie. It was the first time in so long that I have been able to enjoy myself. We also each bought some music. I have my new tape on right now.

Dad is opening up more—he is beginning to talk. He said he is lost now. He misses you. He is afraid of doing what he needs to do for his own fulfillment. He seems sad. What can we do for him? I wish you were here for him. I know he would be so happy if you were alive. It is hard to have a broken heart. I somehow feel stronger, but I cannot figure out why. Are you helping me? There is this movement now regarding angels. It seems as if every magazine or book I pick up has some type of article about angels.

The minute I saw you, I said, "There is my angel." I did not know at the time that you would die, but you were my angel from the beginning, and I loved you from the first moment. I have my most favorite picture of you in front of me, one from the first day of your life. You are so beautiful! I could not believe you could be so gorgeous. But you were, and I cried when I saw you. Why did things have to work out this way? I accept things more now, but there are days I would give my eyeteeth to have you with me.

There was a time after we found out how sick you were that I sobbed and cried and cursed God. I played music at the highest volume to try and let something else penetrate. But this pain was swirling inside of me, jabbing me like a knife would. It felt as if the pain took over and I went through a dreamlike state with sleepless nights and tears—so many tears.

Sweetheart,   November 26, 1994

Hello, angel. How are you doing? I have so much to tell you. Dad and I are doing much better. We are actually talking and feeling close. He is off his trip about me. Or himself. He is the old guy we know and love. We both miss you dearly. I talk of you every day. Yesterday I had a hard day. It was my birthday and I felt fine, and then I missed you something fierce. I got so sad. I thought of how we could have been so close. How we could have been together. How beautiful you were and still are.

Lately, some things have weighed on my mind. First of all, the day you died I woke up from a dream with this euphoric feeling of extreme well-being. Although I could not remember the dream, the feeling stayed with me. This feeling was like none that I had ever felt before. I felt as if I could soar. It only lasted for seconds.

I realized then that you were at the hospital, still struggling. I had to take a tranquilizer before I went to see you. When I got to the hospital, I rushed to see you. The minute I walked through the doors, your breathing started getting worse. I went to a private room with you, and Grandma Sara came in to see us. Your breathing was more difficult, and I went to a place inside myself where there was no time, there was nothing but pain. I did not know what to do except hold you. There were no rules, no laws of love to follow. Your dying was so real. A sword had pierced my heart. I hung on and you lay in my arms. Daddy made me go lie down. Forty-five minutes later, he came and told me you had died. I thought he had made it up, that it could not have happened. Grandpa Cole, my father, was holding you when I came into the room and saw you. I must have started sobbing because Grandpa made a weird sound in his throat when he saw my distress. Your color was gone, but you still had this golden hue. I kept holding you and rocking you. Oh, Gracie, as I write this I am sobbing. It's so hard to relive all of this and not have you. Death is so final.

Three months after your death, I went to see this astrologer that everyone at work has gone to see. Her name is Pat. I told her about the feeling I had awoke with the morning you died, this euphoric feeling. I could not understand this at all and I have often thought of it. Why?

Before I go on, I must tell you that I had never told Pat about your death or that I even had had a child. I had barely gotten through the door (I could tell that she was a little nervous), when she said that she had seen, through this formation of the stars, that I had this particular thing resembling the Greek Demeter story where Demeter (a Greek goddess) had lost her daughter, Persephone, to the underworld. I started crying and told her that you had recently died. Pat said she knew I had been through something traumatic. She told me that I had lived an actual archetype. That I had lived my worst fear, that this was a universal fear of all parents. When I asked her about the euphoric feeling the morning of your death, she said that it was the feeling you had when you met God and left the earth. I felt this rush of understanding at that moment. I felt and knew that she was right. That emotion I'd had was unlike any I had ever known. It was so powerful. If only I had known that you would have felt that only hours later . . .

Darling, I must go. This was all so much to write. To actually write of your death is . . .

Darling Angel,   November 29, 1994

Tonight I finished a picture book of your life that Dad had started. It was so interesting to see myself pregnant with you in the spring and summer, and then to see your first days of life. I came across a picture tonight of you looking at me and actually seeing and knowing me. It made me so happy. At the end, it was so hard for you to see, and I worried so much about how you were feeling. Were you in pain? To feel you might suffer was the worst feeling for me. I cried, Gracie, again, so hard. But so much of this was the reality of your life. And it was such a valiant life. So complete. So real. I saw in those photographs how strong you really were and how much personality you had. There was so much life in you. You gave me so much happiness, and now I don't know how my new life will be.

Daddy is not doing well, himself. He does not want to talk about things, like your death, or even his job at times. He keeps things within, but I sense these things. I want to talk, while he is a man of few words. Yet, when he does say something, it is always with so much sensitivity. Daddy has a need to stay what I would term "balanced." He prizes the fact that he can be even-keeled. I, on the other hand, do not mind going into my feelings. I let my feelings become a part of me, but maybe too much. In this way, your father and I do balance each other out—I can take him to the stars by my excitement, and he can make sure my feet stay on the ground by his sense of balance. Right now, though, we are both off center.

He is quiet and he is trying not to smoke. We both, unfortunately, started after the fifth surgery. The pressure was too intense. But more on that later. I do love you, Sweetie.

Well, honey,   December 12, 1994

This will be a Christmas that you will not be with us, and I, personally, will miss you. So much reminds me of you. This is the first time that I have been able to write lately. The pace is picking up.

Amanda just dropped something off at my door. (She says it came from you.) It reads:

> *A Memory Box To Mom*
>
> *From Grace Love*
> *Here's some of Bobs fur*
> *I got & fools gold my sister Amanda got me.*
> *please thank Amanda for letting me watch her*
> *movie Monkes trouble and allso for letting me have*
> *naps with Bob on her coutch!*
> *LOVE,*
> *GRACE LOVE*
>
> *I love you Mom*
> *I love you Dad*
> *I love you Sis*

Wasn't that sweet? Even though it was not from you exactly, it was from you in so many ways. Love comes out when you least expect it.

Your sister is something else. I remember how she wanted to read stories to you at the hospital. Both Amanda and I kept reading and reading to you, hoping you could hear us. My favorite story was *Goodnight Moon,* and Amanda's was *The Runaway Bunny,* both by Margaret Wise Brown. I feel my throat getting tight again.

I am just so grateful for what I have. I love this room, honey. This room is your room, really. It would have been the nursery. It is just so sweet. I have my books close by, in this little wooden bookcase. Everything is in a wonderful neutral cream color—it is such a simple room. There is also the writing desk I got from my grandmother Sylvia. Every piece of furniture in here was chosen with tenderness. I didn't know that was happening when I started redoing the room—but it has. I didn't even know that I would write in here, of all places. But I do.

I just feel love when I come in here. I calm down. And it seems so appropriate that I feel so close to you when I am writing. You are my angel! I love you with all of my heart and I will never stop. Yet each time I write, it is as if all these emotions that I have bottled up come rushing out and the tears start. I think that I am living some way fully in life and then I realize that I really am not, that a part of me will always belong to you. And that this wound will not really be gone. And would I want it to be? Would I want it to be?

Dear Daughter,   December 20, 1994

It is five days before Christmas. I have most of my

shopping done and that feels good. I have been in a funk in some ways. Amanda's other mom had a baby girl last week and I felt so bad that we did not have you. All these emotions came out again, and I have had trouble keeping the tears back. I hate myself for having these feelings, but I do. And it hurts. I am so angry that I can hardly stand it!

It is funny how you can get stuck on one emotion and have it consume your being for that time. I can really understand how people who have been hurt severely in their lives just build up these walls or let hate stop them from life. It is so hard for me to accept my base emotions. I feel ugly for not being able to carry on. Your father has a hard time with me when I really feel. He wants to fix me, and I cannot stand that. He blames himself and wants me to have a happy life; he wants to give me all that is within his power.

Those thoughts are so beautiful. But when you feel, you feel, and I miss you and wish that things were different. I want you to have a life with me! I want you to have Christmas with the family! I want to dress you in little dresses and comb your hair. I want to hold you and not have you leave me. I want you, Grace! I want you so much. I want to smell your baby smell on my hands and know that you are in the next room when I hear you cry. How can a person want something so much and not have it be?

When I finally got the courage to have you, because I loved your father so much, it turned out so tragically. Is God punishing me? Why could I not have the child I wanted? Why? I write and write and that is all that I have. I do not have my child, just computer keys. Please come to me, Grace. Somehow, please. Let me wrap my love around you. Let me hold you once again. Let me be the mother I could not be when you were on this earth. I was so stressed out when you were alive. It wasn't who I really am. I was just a shell of someone who was trying to hang on. I'm sorry, darling. I'm so sorry.

Grace,   December 21, 1994

I miss you, honey. I dare not even think of how old you would be now. Let's see—I guess I will go into this feeling, you know how I get. You would have been five months old, almost to the day. Five months! Oh, if I let myself dream, to think of you on this earth, I kind of torture myself. You know that I have to pause for long moments as I write this. Sometimes I just find myself looking out the window of this room, but I do not even see what I am looking at. I've got to start leaving a Kleenex box in here. I never know when the tears will start.

Across the room, I see the tear-shaped antique bottles that I am collecting. The story goes that in the Middle East, when a man left his love, she would collect her tears in a bottle. When he would come home to rejoin his love, he would see how many tears she had cried in the bottle. Well, I did not know the story behind this when I began collecting these bottles. I just saw how beautiful they were and I knew they would be perfect for your room.

And then I read the insert that told their meaning. They were made to collect tears. It seemed so appropriate for my love for you.

Dear Gracie,   December 22, 1994

Well, I am having a bad evening. I went to get Amanda at her day care and everyone thought I was her other mother. They wished me "happy new motherhood." It seemed like a cruel joke. It is so hard for me at times because Amanda has her feelings and I have mine. Amanda has her feelings of excitement for her new sister and I have feelings of envy. I want excitement and happiness too.

I wanted to have a sister for her. You were her sister and now you are gone. And she has a new sister. And I think she has forgotten you, even though it is so hard for a child. I have so many base, ugly feelings about this whole thing. What can I do?

Dear Grace,   December 31, 1994

It is New Year's Eve, and Dad and I are home. We decided not to go out tonight, but that is okay. We need some quiet time. Last year we went to a little French restaurant in the Cathedral Hill area in St. Paul. Little did I know that the dress I wore that night was the one that I would wear at your funeral.

You know that I think of you every day. It has been hard for me at times. Very hard. I look at your picture, and I ask why. It is almost as if I still cannot believe this has happened. Sometimes your memory is not quite as clear as at other times. Sometimes the pain of your loss gets fainter, and I feel as if I am losing you. I know, if I have the pain, that things are so real then. Oh, Grace, Dad and I talked about having another baby last night. But no one could replace you. No one. I am not ready yet. And I am scared, but maybe someday it would be possible. We love you so much. So much. Is it the right thing to do?

I love you, darling girl. I love you. With all my heart,

Hello sweetheart,   January 8, 1995

How are you? Mom has been thinking of you in the best of ways. Guess what? I had Sandy over. She was your night nurse. She is the most wonderful of people, and we had such a nice visit. She knew how special you were. I thought that most new mothers had this feeling about their child, but when I talk to her, I know that you really were different. You had the power to move people, honey. Sandy told me that all the nurses had said how wonderful you were and what a good little girl you were to take care of. Oh, sweetheart, I can't believe that you could be that good after so many surgeries. But you were, and I was so proud of you. And I bet that you are flying around right now just being the most precious angel. There was nothing but goodness about your life. You were pure.

The day of your funeral, I was facing the audience—it was right at the end when things were wrapping up—and I looked up and saw an angel hovering by the far corner of the chapel. I knew that it had to be you. The robes this angel wore looked too big for it, and everything was fuzzy for me because I had tears in my eyes. But I did see that this angel had wings and that the wings had light blue along the edges. The robes were of an antique fabric, like old silk. Well, I blinked a few times and I kept seeing the angel, but on the third blink it went away. Was that you? I told people about this right away, and they must have thought I was crazy, but I did not care. Especially on the day of your funeral. But I thought that maybe God had let you just take a look at us when you were whole and could see and understand. If this is what happened, then I know that you saw how much Dad and I loved you and how much everyone loved you.

Honey, that chapel was so packed. There was standing room only. The medical staff came, the nurses, friends of the family, and work friends. It was amazing. Love came out of every corner of the room. The music was beautiful. Daddy sang "Amazing Grace" a cappella. I do believe that you wanted me to see you, and that at that moment, you did show yourself to me! But I don't know why those robes were so big for you. It's like you had to grow into them or something.

This brings to mind my friend Julie, from the university. We had grown very close, and even before we shared our pregnancies, I had this connection with Julie—this unspoken bond. I knew it and I knew that she knew it. She has been my pillar of strength, and we don't even need words to understand what the other one is feeling. I told her about your death the other day. We were at a conference for work, and I just started talking at lunch. It is so hard for me to speak of the painful parts of this. I cried again, another trait I have picked up. But Julie, she sat and listened and was so present. I can't put words on the feeling I get from sharing time with her. It is truly so special.

Darling girl, I must go now. I may write again today, but there are things I have to get to. You can see that I have not talked to you in a while and that I have had a lot of things to say. I feel so much better, Grace! It is as if I am healing, and I cannot believe it! Thank you, little one. . . .

Dearest Gracie,   January 23, 1995

I have not written to you in so long. Dad, Amanda, and I got back from a Florida vacation. Dad thought it would really be nice to get away for a while. I want you to know that we had such a nice time. Amanda stayed with your grandparents, Jim and Nancy, so that Dad and I had time for ourselves, at least at night. The beaches went on for miles. The water was an emerald green and the waves would hit the shore and make beautiful white sea froth. It was lovely. Dad and I both felt our cares melting away. We laughed and loved and became very close again. When I can make your father laugh, it makes me so happy. We were so silly. On the last day, we were at the beach by ourselves and I tried to do a rap song for Dad (to make him laugh) and I totally screwed it up. My rhythm is not the best in music.

It just got me to thinking that maybe you would have been like me. Amanda is like your father, and when I am who I am, I am probably quite impish and funny, and serious at times and very searching and focused inward toward bigger things. Evolving is important to me. I wondered, would you have had my temperament?

These things all came to my mind and then I thought that I will never know the answer. I thought of how brave you had been during your lifetime—how incredibly strong—and I knew that you did have some of me in you. You had my strength to live. I started crying, and the tears would not stop. Dad was sitting by me, and we were looking out at the ocean, and these tears were streaming down my face, and the wind was blowing hard. I could not stop crying. Dad always feels so bad when I get like that. I kept thinking, *I can't believe you died when I didn't even get to know you.* But somehow I knew you in my own fashion. I knew when you looked at me that you knew me, that you recognized my voice, and that we had shared something rare. We knew. We shared life and death. But honey, I wish it could have been different. I really miss you. With you, I came in touch with that lost side of me, that side that you will always have.

I wonder how women and men who have lost their children survive? I was getting ready for work recently when I heard a news report about the anniversary of the space shuttle that had blown up nine years ago, the Challenger. The mother of the teacher on board was talking about all the good things that had come about because of her daughter's death, and I could not imagine this, that a person could be that healed.

I realize that I have to look at the fact that you have died. Everyone but me has accepted this. People say move on, but it is so hard for me. Last night I was driving home in my car and the tears started, and I began to moan and cry just like I used to do when you were alive. It is such a pitiful sound when you hear yourself make those noises. I realized that we as humans are so close to animals, really. Pain is pain. And the sounds of pain are universal and cannot be claimed by one species or another as only their own.

I must go, honey. I am so tired, and I have to work tomorrow.

Dear Gracie,   January 27, 1995

Another one of those days . . . work and going home. I wonder what I am to do with my life? What will I do? Where am I left? What is left for me? What? "How can I forget you?"—that is what Betty Carter is singing just at the moment. I feel kind of listless and mad, and I have a hard time thinking of what I have lost. If all matter is energy, then where is your energy? When I feel good about things, I feel as if you are so close to me, and when I am discouraged, you seem so far away. Why is this? When will this feeling of melancholy leave me? Right now, I have some incense burning and I have lit a candle; I am trying to create a loving environment for myself, but

I really do not have a lot of energy. Grief is such a strange thing. Does it ever pass?

Dear Daughter,   January 30, 1995

I am feeling better than the last time I wrote. I was feeling so low. I really do not know what it was, except that it probably had something to do with you. Dad and I kind of had it out because I felt that he was not really helping out around the house. I would ask him to do something, and he would say he would, and then he'd just blow it off and never do it. At times, he is very threatened by who I am. This was one of those times. I think it's because I have been carrying on and organizing things, and he cannot stand it.

He has a problem in that he hears so much criticism when there is a request made of him. I, on the other hand, have it totally together—wrong! I have my issues too, which you would have seen, had you lived. My big issues are that I am somewhat of a perfectionist and have control issues. I do think that I have good ideas and that I often see solutions quite easily. Your father has wonderful qualities also. He can say he is sorry, he can be as gentle and as soothing as anyone I know, and he is incredibly bright and insightful. But I do not know how much of a worker he really is. Oh well . . .

Dear Grace,   February 1995

I have been having so many unusual dreams lately. Recently I had a dream in which I was taking care of a black man's child. In fact, I even nursed this child. He was the most caring man I had ever met. We did not talk with our mouths; everything was understood through our minds. I kept feeling nothing but love from him. He told people, "Look how she has loved my daughter." He had the most loving of eyes. The next scene, I was in a doorway with this man, and he was holding my hand. He was in a wheelchair. He looked up at me, again with such incredible tenderness, it made me want to weep. I had never felt this kind of love before. I knew if I loved him, I would never be the same again.

Well, because so much is happening on this level, I had to tell someone. So at work, I started relating this dream. Julie almost dropped what she was carrying. She said that she had a dream the week before with a black man in it too, and in the second half he was in a wheelchair! None of us could believe this! She and this man also communicated through their minds. The nature of each dream was different, but Julie also felt love from the man. I know this is because of you, Gracie. But what does it mean?

Darling,   February 22, 1995

You would have been seven months old, today. Seven months! Julie brought in Peter today, and he was so sweet. An angel, just like you. His energy is wonderful. It gives me so much solace to see where he is in life and to know there is so much love.

I am filled with love tonight. We had a school problem with Amanda, and we worked it out. She is so close to me and we both know it. We have this unspoken bond that I treasure. How could I have made it without her? Or is it you working your magic? I feel as if you have left me somehow. I don't know why. It is as if you have crossed to the other side. That makes me sad. Have you? I look at the computer screen and it is dark, not glowing like it used to be. Remember? Were you trying to communicate with me and I was not ready for it? Well, I am now. I love you, darling, and I cry for you. Don't you see my tears? Don't you know what is in my heart, or do you just see my actions and what is not in my heart? Don't leave me, Sweetheart. Are you fading into a place I do not know? Or will you reveal yourself to me? Let me know.

I am your mother, always.

Darling Grace,   March 4, 1995

I love your name so much. I have been ill this past week and haven't felt like doing anything, even reading. Then I started reading this angel book that I got for Christmas. I wonder if you are an angel. . . . They say angels are a different species from humans, "messengers of God," not on the physical plane as we humans are but on the spiritual plane. We are all energy. I know that your energy is somewhere, and I know that if I were more evolved, I could accept that you are gone. I understand that the energy is what is important and that it is love. Grace, I can grasp this intellectually at times, but there are other times when I would give anything to have you on the physical plane.

I wonder if I am being punished for something that happened that I am unaware of. They say in this book that there are no accidents, that everything is for a bigger reason, and that to get it, you have to go through it. But in my usual, questioning way, I wonder why. I read all this stuff, and it sounds so good, but then it comes right down to the fact that I simply miss you. And I long for you—to hold you. There will always be a hole in my heart.

One good thing came out of this reading. You know that I can be quite unbending if I think I might be right. Well, I have spent two and a half years trying to convince your father to "see things my way," and then all of a sudden, I realized that he will never change; he is who he is. And I am who I am. Acceptance is the only way. It was really a breakthrough for me. It is so simple, yet so hard. What I love about your father is also what I have the hardest time with. And so it is. So it is.

I guess the key is to let go. Like a cool summer breeze, let the airflow take you there, and you cannot fight it.

Gracie,   March 1995

The strangest thing happened on my way in to work, on the freeway. A white bird flew right in front of my windshield. It was right smack dab in front of me. I worried for a moment that I might hit it, but it started ascending with its head cocked to the side, just like pictures of the American eagle or the phoenix. It was so close that if I could have put my hand through the window, I could have touched it. I have driven this route hundreds of times, and a bird like this, let alone a white bird, has never come this close. I was so rattled by the time I got to work that I had to tell Julie about this. I think it might have been a dove. But why a dove?

Dearest Daughter, March 1995

Gracie, I have to let you know what is going on at work. All of us—Julie, Margaret, and I—have been reading books. I got a book from your Grandma Love about angels, by Sophy Burnham. I had read her book *Revelations* recently, and then all of a sudden, this book was mailed to me from your grandmother. I brought it in to work one day to show everyone. When I was done with it, Julie read it, then Margaret. We have started passing books around. We each kind of have our own bent, but sometimes our tastes intersect. It is so much fun discussing things and sharing ideas. We have even begun comparing notes about our dreams. Julie has always been the avid dreamer in the group, but Margaret and I are beginning to notice our dreams more. There is this feeling of shared events going on now. I am beginning to trust and open up a little more. I have to do something, Grace, otherwise this pain would somehow take over.

I have to go, Honey.

Darling Grace, March 14, 1995

So much has been going on since I last wrote, a lot of

emotional and spiritual activity, with dreams and sharing with Margaret and Julie. First off, I should tell you that Daddy and I are very much in love. Something short of a miracle has taken place in love with your father and me—a deeper understanding of sorts. Although I always knew how much Daddy loved me, I have never felt or seen it more than now. I knew it intellectually, but not from the heart. I changed my approach with him, and I have been getting all this love back. You know how defensive I can be. You know how defensive he can be. We both wanted to defend our place in our lives together, and now I have let it go. He is who he is. And I am who I am. In certain ways, he can grow through my knowledge, and in certain ways, I can grow through his. So much of this revolves around acceptance. But I had to let him in.

When I speak of letting him in, I realize there is another spirit that is entering me. . . . I have been reading these angel books, and I guess I am so open or receptive after your birth and death that, through a series of situations, I have started thinking a lot about God and angels and you and your spirit. I have mentioned before that when I have been in tremendous emotional pain, this computer has glowed at night. I went to turn it off the first time and discovered it was not on. There was only a glowing computer screen. This has happened at least six times. Was that you? When I realized that this had happened, I just went to bed, until it happened the next time. I had prayed that you would reveal yourself to me as an angel or something, and then this started happening. The computer has been our only way of communicating. I know this. I have gotten frightened by this, and I have not known how to react. But I am working on my fear.

I have been having dreams; some of them seem to have spiritual symbolism in them. I also read this book about a woman who had a near-death experience. I know, dear daughter, that you are in the most loving of hands and that you are pure and chose to come here for a reason. Your purpose touched so many people around you. Oh, please, know how much I loved you and still love you. You may have awakened a love in me for God and myself that was in hiding for so long. It is as if I am seeing love in the smallest and simplest of places. I always thought that I was pretty spiritual in a modern sense, but ever since your birth, when I have heard love songs, I think only of my love for you, not the typical love. Now I hear songs about being blinded by the light and love, and I think of God. I wonder if I ever was truly spiritual in the right sense—if I have ever truly loved myself and God. It is as if I am being awakened.

I have read that there is free will, and that on this earth we can choose to use it as we see fit. This is God's promise to us. But if we do need anything, all we have to do is ask. When was the last time that I prayed other than when I was pregnant? At the first sign of problems, I started to pray. But I didn't when I thought everything was fine.

Did I thank God for anything before all this? I think maybe twice a year, if that. I was so out of touch with everything. I thought that I was a decent person, but maybe I was mean and horrible. Was I missing something? Was I too selfish and did I only think of myself, ultimately? (I just took time out to look at your pictures and I had to cry again. You were so wonderful.) I am ashamed that I worried about how we would care for you. I worried that we might not have the money or we would become so tired that things would fall apart, and yet, that too was simply selfish on my part. I am ashamed as I write this. I have learned so much since we were together, but was it because of your death? And did I cause you to suffer?

If I only knew then what I know now—that love can cure anything, that all of life is about love and hope and faith. But darling, know one thing: I will always feel this love and loss for you. No one has affected my life as you do and have. And if I caused any of this to happen to you and you died because you did not feel enough love from me, then I do not know how I can bear that thought. Oh, Darling, I love you with all of my heart, and if you were here I would show you, but please know this. I love you.

Darling,   March 26, 1995

I have not written to you in a while. It is not because I haven't been thinking of you, though. Almost every minute is taken up with thoughts of you—while working, driving, looking at the trees, feeling the spring winds.

All these things bring back memories of when we were together while I was carrying you. Remember when I carried all those boards from under the bushes in the backyard? They had been left by the former owners of our house. The yard had looked so bad after the winter, until we started picking it up. Just you and me. Dad kept looking from the window in the house, holding his coffee cup. I would look up, and there he would be, looking at me. I must have been seven months pregnant. It was then, in the spring, that I really started loving you. I felt good. Strong. The sun would warm my skin and I would feel my muscles working and you moving. I knew you felt strong then. We worked as one. We were quite a team. I felt nothing could have been sweeter. You inside me, the love I felt for your father, the spring sunshine, and the dirt on my hands. I felt so alive! Was that what you did for me? Open me up to life? Make me feel more alive? What, Gracie, what? You live inside me even now! And in my stubbornness, I don't want to let you go.

Spring is coming again and you are not here. I have only the trees and the grass. I keep raking because it reminds me of a time when I was so happy—waiting for you to arrive into this world. When I look up to the window that would have been yours, I feel empty, and sometimes tears sting my eyes. When I hear the same birds that sang to me as I worked last year sing to me now, I realize this is how it is. That you won't be coming. That I cannot turn back time. That I must carry you in my heart. But I know that you were my deepest love and my deepest pain. The wind carries you to me, softly. As your spirit swirls around me, I am filled with the wonder that every mother has for her child. Although I cannot hold you in my arms, you fill me with your purity. And I thank God for that.

Dearest Grace,   March 28, 1995

I have to tell you that things are happening so quickly to me now. I'll try to explain.

Ever since the day that you died, the day I had that dream feeling of euphoria before I realized you were still so ill and suffering, I have had dreams, had thoughts, been filled with love, watched my life change . . . and now I have had the experience of leaving my body. One night I was sleeping and I felt myself leaving my body. About halfway up from the bed to the ceiling, I got scared and went back into my body with a *whoosh*. I still felt as if I had the same personality, but I was not in my body. Well, I just told Dad about this and he said that it was not a bad thing, just to let these experiences happen naturally. But I am one for naming things, and I have to put words on some things. It gives me strength and comfort. But. . . .

(The cursor begins to scroll through all I have written.)

I I.
SEARCHING

QUESTIONS

Gracie,   April 1995

   I don't know quite how to put this, but I will do the best I can. The last time I wrote to you, on March 28, something occurred. In fact, I have to write this by hand because the computer is on the fritz. I hesitate because I am searching for words at the moment. . . .

   Let me start at the beginning of the night. I had told Dad about these out-of-body experiences I had been having. The time was right, and I was feeling so safe and close to your father. We were both sharing on this wonderful level. You know what a good listener he can be. I remember we were making spaghetti, and I was just putting the noodles in the boiling water, when your father told me he had a gift for me. He pulled this tape out of his briefcase—it was called *Calling All Angels.* He knows how much angels mean to me now, because of you.

After dinner, Daddy and Amanda were watching television, and I ran upstairs to write to you. I put the tape in and began writing. Your father then came upstairs, during a commercial, to give me a kiss. Grace, it was a wonderful kiss.

As your father left the room, I resumed typing. As I did, the cursor on the computer screen began going through my writing on its own. I became alarmed and tried to gain control of the cursor, when your father's words rang in my ears. He had just told me that the out-of-body experiences were nothing bad and that I should be "natural" about them. I kept trying to control the cursor, but then I stopped to see what would happen if I didn't. My heart, by this time, was in my throat. I could hear the blood pounding in my ears. The cursor disappeared, and the letters of my writing began to glisten, as if they had some sort of diamond quality. Then I watched as the computer scrolled upward, through all I had written. The cursor stopped at a point in my writing where I had told you that I knew we could communicate like this, through the computer.

Gracie, at that moment, the cursor began flashing normally again, I had an intense desire to sob. I was filled with an awe of some sort. I began to cry, but I couldn't define what I was feeling. Because I could not understand what had just happened, I got down on my knees and said a prayer. I then ran and told your father. He said that there was probably some type of energy surge or something. The whole evening I felt somewhat dazed. I kept thinking, *How can this be?* I knew in my heart it wasn't a power surge. It had something to do with you.

Darling Grace,   April 1995

I have to tell you that I had a dream in which I saw five huge angels in the sky, flying around in robes. In the next scene of the dream, I saw myself landing on the ground. My skin was flesh colored, and I had wings that were also of a flesh tone. I saw my feet touch the ground, as if I were landing lightly.

Gracie, I have also had a dream in which I saw the Star of David, and another in which I saw a multipetaled white flower over my head. I found out later that this was the lotus flower, which in Hinduism means divine energy and divine grace. What is going on?

Grace, it seems as though I am coached by someone in my recent dreams. I hear a voice, but I do not see anyone. Yet, it feels as if I am learning something. I keep wondering why I am getting these religious symbols. And are all the religions connected somehow?

Julie has also had the Star of David in a dream, so it is not just me. Is it because we were pregnant together?

Dearest Daughter, April 1995

I have some concerns again. I went into my computer after this last episode I told you about. I wanted to write to you, and when I opened the program, a file was high-lighted and the warning bell sound on my computer was chiming again and again. I opened the file, and saw that it was a note I had written to Margaret in January, after I read the mystery novel that she is working on. The whole time, the signal bell was chiming every second!

It got me all rattled again. I tried to write something, and the letters kept going to the beginning of whatever I typed. Finally, I turned the computer off. I told your father again, and he said that the computer was malfunc-tioning. I know this is not so. But I am wondering if you are trying to tell me something and I cannot understand. I am concerned about this, Grace. Why can't I under-stand? This bothers me so much.

Dearest Grace, April 1995

When I was eight years old, exactly the age of Amanda, my mother lost a child, my brother Matthew. He had something totally unrelated to your condition and he only lived four days. At that time, people did not deal with death in the way they do now. Mothers could not see their newborns if they were really sick in the hospitals. So Grandma never saw her child—ever. She lived with that loss for years. When you came into her life, Grace, you were a child—a grandchild—whom she *could* hold and comfort, as she couldn't hold and comfort Matthew.

Grace, Grandma has been so affected by your life and death. She cries every time I bring up your name. Yet, ironically, with all that emotion, she has a very logical way of looking at a problem. I have always felt comforted by this. So I knew I could confide in her. I knew I had to talk to her about what has happened to me recently. I drove to her house last night.

I told the computer story—how I had been writing to you still, how the computer screen had been glowing at night, how the cursor moved by itself. I related the out-of-body experiences; I even mentioned the similar dreams that Julie and I have had. My mother just listened. I also told her about the dove flying in front of my windshield.

Grandma started crying. There was no judgment coming from her, only support. She told me that her best friend also had seen a white bird outside her window after her mother had died. Grandma said that it was a sign. I kept wondering, *Why is it that people never talk about these signs?* And yet it seems that everyone who has lost a loved one believes in some type of connection. Some sign that will keep them connected. Is this based on trust?

Gracie Darling,   April 1995

I am sinking. I keep trying to get into my computer, but I cannot get it to work. I know that this is connected to you. Your father still thinks the computer is just on the fritz. He told me to get it looked at, so that I won't get hurt if it is not you. Gracie, I keep trying to understand what you may be trying to tell me. I am worried that maybe I have done something wrong in my life, and God is mad at me or something. I am even thinking that my reputation, along some line, has rubbed off on you in the heavenly realm. I am so frustrated that I can't get the computer to write. What if you need my help? You are pure, Grace—I know this has to do with me. If I have done anything to tarnish your reputation in heaven, I'll die. Grace, I have so many questions. And no answers.

Dear Gracie,   May 1995

I look at my life now and I wonder, *How can all of this be happening?* As you know, I have begun sharing things with Julie, but after the dove incident, Margaret was brought into these discussions. She is Catholic and is more famil- iar with religious symbols, or at least she knows where to look for information on them.

When I asked her about the meaning of the dove, she came back the next day and said that it represented the Holy Spirit or the Eternal Mother! I almost fell off my chair. Margaret continually strikes me as so steadfast and gentle; Julie, as full of such tenderness. Both of them are so different from myself. I have had to open up to them, Gracie, because I cannot hold these events inside.

Well, the other day Margaret called me up at work, from her home, and told me she thinks she has spoken to an angel—her angel! This really came out of nowhere. I had no idea she was even thinking of doing something like this.

I was somewhat shocked; I even felt jealous. But with everything that has happened lately, I am beginning to feel that anything may be possible. When I told Julie about this angelic communication, she wanted to go over to Margaret's the next day. Margaret has been home from work lately, getting her home ready to sell. Although I responded willingly, I only halfheartedly went.

Gracie, we sat at Margaret's kitchen table on this beautiful spring day, and Margaret told us what her angel had said. Julie and I were all full of questions. "How could this happen?" "How do you do it?" Things of that sort. When I read the words on Margaret's computer, I was overwhelmed. There was so much truth in the words, however they may have come. I started getting quiet.

Grace, I have fear in me. This is bordering on things I do not understand. Margaret has been able to connect to this angelic realm, but I cannot write to you, and you *are* an angel. I feel this verifies the fact that something is very wrong with me.

Several days later, Julie asked Margaret to talk to the angel (now named Peace) for her. I felt myself withdrawing. Although I had shared the aspect of physical events with these women, I had not shared my growing fear. I kept feeling so flawed. But this was my secret.

I know that I am rambling now, but I must get this out. The next day, Margaret came in with news for Julie, from her angel. Margaret then turned to me and said that she had felt that I had also given her permission to speak to *my* angel. This was my worst nightmare! Margaret's first words with her angel, Peace, had rung with such truth that I knew the angels would spill the beans about me and let everyone know what a horrible person I am. Why else could you have died?

Margaret then went on to tell me what my angel had said. He said he missed me or something like that. I took this to be a sure sign that I was somehow out of circulation in this angelic realm. Gracie, I am just sinking here. I had to leave work.

I tell you, first you die, then all this starts happening, and I am supposed to make sense out of it. Isn't your dying enough? I just cried in the backyard. Margaret even said that my angel seemed "stern." They had to put the tough one with me! Gracie, I am convinced that I am a tough case for anyone—even your father. It's probably better you are with God than with a mother like me.

I know this sounds fierce, but it is how I feel. And I am stuck with this churning in my insides. Gracie, I am sinking.

Dear Grace,   May 1995

We are a couple of weeks into this angel writing of Margaret's. Remember how I told you that I had to leave work after Margaret talked to my angel? Well, the next day, on my way in to work, I got behind a car that was

filled with balloons, and one read "To Cheer You Up!"
The whole back window was covered with these balloons,
but the only balloon with writing on it was directly in
front of me. I thought that the car would go on to the
university hospital, but it didn't. It turned where I usually turn into the parking lot. I couldn't miss it.

Dear Grace,   May 24, 1995

I had another dream last night. In this dream I saw a
woman, the mother of a friend who had died. The dead
woman was laid out on a sidewalk, and everyone was
walking around her. I kept asking people when this
woman would be buried. No one would answer me.
Then, I was looking from behind this scene at an incredibly magnificent dog—a German shepherd—sitting
beside a mound of dirt. The dog was so beautiful. It was as
if he were watching over this pile of dirt.

Well, I told your father about the dream, and I said, "We
have to bury Grace." You see, Gracie, we have your ashes
at home. I wanted to bring you home somehow, to be
with me. But I think that now is the time that we have to
do this. Daddy doesn't even question these dreams. He
just said, "Okay."

I called your Grandma Sara and there is a plot in
Austin, Minnesota, where the rest of the family is buried.
I think that is the best place. Julie told me that when we
buried you, she wanted to be there, because she felt so bad
about not coming to your funeral.

I spoke to your father, and we both agreed that we would all say a few words by the burial site. I just want to keep this simple.

Dear Daughter,   May 1995

I could not believe it, but I got so nervous about the burial. It rained cats and dogs that day. I had written something to read to you, and I brought that little teddy bear from Amanda to put in the grave with you. You were buried by my brother Matthew. My parents, Deb Bohnen, and Julie and her husband, Kelly, were all there. Margaret has had all this stuff going on with selling her house and her daughter's graduation, so it was just this small group. My sister, Liz, and brother, Charlie, also could not be there.

We stood in the rain, under umbrellas. The wind kept whipping the pages I had written to you, and the ink ran down them as I read the words. It was Memorial Day weekend. Everyone said something from their hearts. Dear Julie, who always is so tender, said her words. I know how important that was to her. Then Grandpa interrupted Julie to say his piece—I think to speed things along because of the rain. Even Kelly said something. Deb's words were also so touching. She is the only one of my friends who ever saw you. Time ran out for the others. I kept thinking that time would not run out.

I got so uptight with all of this, just like I did on the day of your funeral service. I felt so wooden inside. I got so cold in the rain. The back of my dress was so wet.

But you know, Grace, I felt then that I had done the right thing. That I had listened to my heart. That it was time to put your body to rest. And for this, Grace, I am grateful.

Gracie,   May 1995

I cry nightly for you. I cry into this space, this nothingness, in hopes that I can somehow find you. I have so much fear in me. I am so worried that I might have mucked things up somehow. Honey, if I have, I didn't mean to. You see, I only have love for you. I cannot express in words how much in love with you I am. And if God can see me, He must know I have done something wrong. I tried to do everything so right. But maybe He thinks that I am too controlling or maybe that I holler too much. But because of how I feel about you, I have to take a chance and have Margaret ask this Peace angel for any word of you. I am scared that he will say I am just somehow no good. You see, Gracie, in my family we are such self-sufficient people. You just don't ask for help unless you are really desperate. But who could I ask for help with this angel stuff anyway? My only hope is Margaret.

Dearest Grace,   June 1995

I finally got the courage to ask Margaret if she could ask this Peace angel about you. I did it today when we were outside talking. I remember Margaret bending her head down, listening to me, letting me say my words. Could she tell how nervous I was? I tried to make the request seem somewhat light but inside, this fear still has a hold on me. In fact, as I write this tonight, I am in more despair than ever. I know Margaret is probably writing right now. I keep thinking of everything that this angel might say. I think of my childhood and how rebellious I was as a teenager. I think of how selfish I have always been and how headstrong. How I try so hard to be good, and then I screw everything up. I think of how many surgeries you had. Were they too many? I think of how Dad and I said "no more" to medical science. Was that right? I think of when I was carrying you . . . what if I walked by a microwave oven and got some type of radiation that hurt you? I am examining everything in my life, Grace, and I keep coming up short. But I have to know. This is an unusual situation, in that I have a friend who is able to do this. And if I have done anything to harm you, or if God is mad at me for some reason, or because of who I am, and I can make it right, then I have to risk everything to find out. Even if the news is bad—which I am almost positive it will be, because of who I am—somehow, Darling, I will help you. I promise to make this right.

I can't write anymore . . .

The next day:

Gracie,

Today at work Margaret brought the news in from her angel about you. We sat out on a veranda by a beautiful fountain. Flowers were everywhere. The sun was so hot. It was Margaret, Julie, and me. Everyone was quiet as I began to read. And Grace, I cried so hard. Tears just ran down my face. I didn't care. This is the first news I have had of you since you died. The first news! Somehow a weight was lifted from me. It was as if I felt the same joy as the first time that I saw you. Peace, the angel, said you are fine! There was a glimmer of light in my heart today. All I needed to know was whether you were okay.

I don't know if Margaret knows what she has done for me today. I don't know if she knows that she has thrown me a life raft. There has never ever been a time in my life where I have ever known such profound gratitude. I kept crying into a napkin. Gracie, I have never received a gift like this. I felt as if Margaret had carried my heart and brought word of you to me. She carried my heart as if it were her own. That is how I felt. That is how much I trusted her.

Gracie, even as I write, I cry, because when a mother loses her child, all she does is look for the reasons why it could have happened. Oh, Gracie! You are an angel! Relief swept over me. I cannot even begin to tell you. It was as if floodgates opened in my heart.

Here is what Margaret's angel, Peace, said:

Mary has only asked because she has reached a point of being where she is ready to know, where she needs to know, where she must know. And I tell you, what Mary needs to know is this: she did everything right. She

89

could not have loved more. She could not have felt more. She could not have withstood more than she did. She had the courage to trust in herself, in her intuition, and she was so right to do so. She was more than right in that there is no right and wrong in following our destiny. She did the only thing she could. And Grace did the only thing she could. Destiny is linked. Not only did Mary live her destiny and Grace live her destiny, but everyone else who was touched by Grace had Grace as part of their destiny, their road to travel, their bridge between the human and the divine. John, Amanda, Sara, the doctors, the nurses, people Mary doesn't even know. Wives, husbands, friends, daughters who heard of Grace's valiant struggle had their destinies touched by Grace.

And Grace, who Mary worried over so, was a being of pure love and pure light. She was all angel. We all have our angelness with us when we are born. We all have a wisdom unrecognizable in the human world. It is the wisdom of remembering. And Grace never forgot! She never forgot for a moment that she was a being of love, a being of one-ness. She knew exactly what she came back to the human form to learn: Love. And she learned it. She learned it so fast and gave it back to the world so fast, there was no need for her to remain in human form. She never spent a moment on this planet when she was not sure, absolutely sure that she was a being of love. Why? Because she lived such a short life? That is part of the reason. The other reason was that she lived her entire life surrounded by love. She did not see tubes or surgical instruments as anything but what they were—instruments of love. She did not see nurses and doctors, she saw beings of love. And because she was wise with the wisdom of remembering, she saw her parents with perfect love. She saw them as the angels they are. She did not see one single imperfection because there was none to see.

Tell Mary that Grace remembered! She left this world a being of light just as she entered it. She had everything you seek! Everything Mary seeks! Why do you suppose she affected people so? They were in the presence of an angel, an angel who never forgot. One who could have turned around and left for home immediately, but who stayed to feel the love around her and to fill those around her with her divine love. Is Grace all right? No one could be better than Grace. Grace Is in divine oneness and love.

And Margaret replied:

Thank you, Peace. I think I can rest assured that you have given Mary what she had to have—understanding and Peace. Thank you. Can I ask one thing more? As you know, ever since Grace, through Grace, because of Grace, Mary has been on a journey of her own. Similar to mine but unique to her. Her own spiritual quest. There have been times on this path when she has been certain Grace spoke with her through her computer. Sometimes the messages have been clear and sometimes they have not been. Sometimes it simply seems as if everything is a frustrating puzzle, as if the computer has gone haywire. She wants to write, she wants to communicate, but she is not only confronted with puzzles, but with an inability to go into her computer and write to her daughter. Can you tell her anything that will help her understand what is happening? Can you give her any assurance about how to know when Grace is reaching out to her? Can you help to solve the riddle?

GRACE

What Mary has received is a reflection of herself. Of her state of being in the Now. Mary has lived through the greatest challenge that humans can face. And she has turned from that challenge, not with bitterness or anger, although these feelings at times fly across her Now, but with hope. What is her hope about? Finding the love she had with Grace. She was so full of Gracie's love that Gracie's loss felt like a great and awful emptiness, an emptiness so great and vast she wasn't sure she was alive. Wasn't sure she could live. How could Grace not return to comfort her and give her hope? How could Grace not return to help her on her journey? Grace is with her every step of the way. Grace leads her to the books, the birds, the signs, the flowers. Grace in her infinite, loving oneness knows the quickest route to welcoming Mary to be with her again.

Why does that way seem full of puzzles and frustrations? Because Mary is full of puzzles and frustrations. This is not something negative I am saying here. I am saying Mary lived through the greatest challenge a human can face and came out of it not with overwhelming anger and bitterness and despair, but with puzzles and riddles. Hurrah for Mary. Because Grace helped her back to remembering more than she has any concept of, she is in a state of puzzles and frustrations. She knows, Knows, more than she ever knew before. She is closer to oneness, closer to her angelhood, closer to the divine all that is than in any lifetime. Yet that Knowing is hidden from her, much like a name you say is on the "tip of your tongue." It is not Grace or Mary's angel, or anyone but Mary who keeps her in the state of frustration.

Again, this is not negative. For most humans, enlightenment is a lifelong occupation. There is a reason for that. There is a reason I only answer the questions you are ready to ask. There is a reason Mary is accessing all that she Knows in a slow and seemingly frustrating way. That reason IS. Like Mary Is. In the Now of life on this planet, Mary *must function day to day: Mary works, Mary interacts with her family, Mary sleeps and dreams and walks and gardens. Perhaps Mary knows that knowing all that Is would make this impossible for her. For the here and now, Mary is wise enough to ask for only that which she can live with in the Now. But it is all there—on the tip of her tongue!*

Why does it seem as if she is asking and searching and not being answered?

Because Mary is in a state of profound forgetting—something she needed to do in order to live with the truth of Gracie's life and death. In your human experience of time, it has been an eternity for Mary since Gracie's death—and an instant. But Mary is not alone. She will never be alone. Ask Mary what she loved about Gracie. Was it her infant face? Her body? Her fingers and toes? Her hair, her eyes? It was everything. And everything Gracie was was love. Pure love. And Mary will never be without it again. No amount of forgetting will rid her of it. There is nothing she can do and nothing she can be that will not carry Grace's love. At this time, it seems a small substitute for the child Mary longed to hold and bring home, but let me tell you, there is nothing greater than this love. Mary is blessed with this love. Mary has touched the divine.

I know these are not the answers in the form you would seek them to be. You want to know if Grace has communicated through the computer. Grace has communicated through love. You want to know what puzzles the computer represents. I tell you the computer represents Mary's puzzlement. You want to know how Mary can communicate. Through love.

All I can tell you is that Gracie is showing Mary the way. How does Mary know that Grace has not just taught her the lesson of asking for help? How does Mary know that This is not more important in the Now than something Grace might have communicated through the computer? If Mary will trust Grace to lead her to the keys, she will eventually be able to unlock all the doors.

Thank you, Peace. Is there anything else Mary should know now?

Tell Mary that she is all right. Tell Mary that everything she does is all right. Tell Mary that Grace and I are smiling.

Dearest Grace,   June 1995

I carry the Peace writing everywhere with me. I keep taking it out of my purse to read it. I showed your father, Grace, I read it to him on the back porch. He said the words were beautiful.

I showed this writing to my sister, Liz, in the powder room of the St. Paul Hotel during my father's retirement party. She started crying too. We both cried. Liz kept saying, "That little angel." I started to tell Liz of all the happenings, of all these connections, one thing after another with Margaret, Julie, and me. It felt so good to talk about them.

TRUSTING

Dearest Grace,   June 1995

As I think more about you and wonder where you are,
I find myself thinking a lot about religion. I mean, what
does religion mean to me? I have never been a church-
goer, but I have always had this kind of strain in me to
embrace certain things, certain beliefs. Does this mean
that I am spiritual? I am wondering what that even means
now. Everything I had once believed seems to be in question. I somehow could never buy into the belief that so
much of religious doctrine surrounded the concept of sin
and punishment—the wrath of God. And how much

fear has been used to motivate in religion. When you are good, you know that you can't keep it up forever, and so you wait for the other shoe to drop. Then there it is— staring you right in the face—sin. It makes me squeamish. And for some reason, it has never added up for me.

I have done so much reading, Grace, on all levels— from mythology to energy to consciousness—trying to make some sense of your death and attempting to figure out where you are. I am probably the only mother in the universe who cannot accept death.

All of this has gotten me to thinking. Margaret is writing like a maniac with this angel, Peace. Each bit of writing holds so much wisdom. A blind man could see that. And this writing is so beautiful; it almost stuns me, it is so much so. I have been thinking, if Margaret can do this, maybe I can too. I have talked to her about how it is done. She simply asks to talk to her angel, and then thoughts come into her mind. I have read enough about energy and consciousness to know that we are all connected through consciousness, through spirit.

Gracie, you see, I still cannot write in the computer, and I just have to express myself. I have always been a word person, a communicator. And so, if somehow you hear me, can you let me know when the time will be right to try this for myself? And if my angel, my guardian can also hear me, I just want you to know that I am thinking of somehow talking to you. I will have to do this by hand, because of the computer. But I figure, thoughts are thoughts. And if somehow you can put your thoughts in my head, then maybe I can write them. I figure it cannot be any different, Grace, than when your father says what I am thinking right at the same moment. He does that all the time. I do believe that these things can happen, and that maybe my angel will help me.

Dearest Angels and Gracie, my daughter,   June 15, 1995

I have thoughts in my mind, and at 12:05 A.M. I felt I had to put them down. I have so many questions. I ask that you help me, my guardian angel or angels, with understanding, if this is possible. I give thanks to all for these thoughts and perceptions. I am feeling words come into me now. I will begin writing. . . .

You live too much on the outside, the external. When you have a bad day, you think you have not done enough. When you have a good day, you have produced. You have worked. But all this lies on the outside of self. Not who you truly are. You feel as if you are dead now, almost wooden. So you tell yourself that this is who I am. But it is not who you really are. You have so much goodness inside. Locked inside.

Today you saw a window in your mind's eye; you even read about the window. This is not a coincidence. This window is open. There is a reason that this thought has come to you. Think of this as a window to the soul, think of transparency, where everything is revealed. Know you are loved. Trust and believe in this love. This pain you cling to will also reveal itself. It will also show you the way, as in any dark room, there is safety. You would reach for the light or let your eyes grow accustomed to the dark. Trust that you can be in the dark room and your eyes can

97

see in this darkness. Trust can lead the way. Trust can lead you to safety. There is nothing in the darkness to hurt you, to scare you. We are here, close to you. Trust that you can trust, that you have permission. This is not punishment for you to realize the darkness, it is only to reveal the light that is there, the safety that is there.

You are so much more than work, than production, but you view yourself in such narrow terms. Stop and Remember, tonight, that if you give to yourself, giving to others will not seem so great, that you will have energy. Remember to simply be. Always be. Do not worry.

These are my thoughts—I want to say angel thoughts. I feel as if I became calm with this writing. Oh, angels and Gracie darling, I love you. Thank you for getting me to write again.

Gracie, June 1995

I tried it! I did it! I tried speaking to my angel. Oh, Gracie, I don't know if what I heard was from my angel, but it was powerful. I could hardly wait to show Julie and Margaret at work the next day. Margaret just beamed when I told her I had done this.

I just sat outside with the journal from Sandy. She gave me this journal the last time I saw her, and there it was in my bookcase, waiting for me to write. So I just began writing, and things started flowing—just flowing. I lost all track of time, and then I read it and felt so connected. I am somewhat hesitant to claim this as angel writing, but I think it might be. This voice seems to have a different tone than that of the Peace angel. I guess when you look at how different Margaret and I are, there's no reason the angels can't have their own way of expressing themselves. I'll include the letters to my angel from now on. . . .

Gracie, I want you to know that I am doing this not to move away from you, but to somehow try and understand things. You will always be a part of these angel letters. I want you to know this. You will always be my special angel. . . .

Dearest Angels and Grace,   June 1995

I have been talking to Margaret about speaking to angels. It appears that when I do this, I do not remember what I have written. I have some vague idea, but nothing in detail. I simply write what comes to me. At times I remember nothing. I have noticed that my handwriting changes when my angel speaks. It still feels as if I should name you, angel. It feels awkward, not knowing what to call you. Margaret had the thought that your name was Trinity when she spoke to you the first time. I keep sensing Bridge. I don't know what to do. More later.

Dearest Angels and Gracie, my angel,   June 17, 1995

Thank you for this breeze, the flowers, the bird singing, the sun. As I sit here this morning, I try to enter a calm.

The word *trust* has been going through my mind all day. What does this mean? Can you help me with trust? My trust in life seems to have been broken now that Grace has died. Everything appears to be in question. Everything. Is it life I do not trust? Is it myself I do not trust? Can I trust what I hear from you? When I woke up today, I looked *trust* up in the dictionary. It meant faith, hope, confidence. Am I on the right track? Can you guide me?

Faith is something that Is. It is there. You search for proof. Yet, many things in life will never be proven. They simply are. What is meaningful to you? Trust? Hope? They are all a part of you that you have denied. You see these qualities in others and believe, but in yourself you doubt that this is possible. You really doubt love of self, of your own worthiness. You have protected self so long because you felt you had to. Self says, I cannot do this any longer. Mind says, I need proof.

But the road is bending, turning for you. The light is there, yet you stumble, you have fear, you do not want to walk, you want to turn back. Realize that you are turning toward life. Do you not see that you are believing? That proof can be disproved? Some things ARE. Proof can be hollow and lead to emptiness. Love is all that is. Love will take you and comfort you when proof stands by you. Your mind fights also to be believed. Take it by the hand. Welcome it. Your mind will believe. You are turning, Mary. You know this.

With knowing, there is hope, faith, and love. Your goodness, which has been denied to you, is bountiful. You have never been able to truly allow this to be revealed. You need this goodness for yourself now. Past hurts and pains have made this so. Believe in this goodness, for it will guide you.

I love you, my dearest angels and Gracie. Thank you. Thank you. Thank you.

What is needed is chosen by you. You choose this to learn. You are communicating. Believe this, Mary. You are seeing. Believe this. You worry about angels' names. They will come in time. Feeling, which is an important realm for you to be in, is here. Know and trust these feelings to guide you to truth. Trust even the pain to be your friend. Because it is. You then can let it be.

The hardest part for you is the "ISness." ISness is simply being. You feel that this is difficult to handle. You fear, and then you doubt. Give yourself credit! You are a well of love. Dip into the well and take a drink! Feel the coolness of the water, savor the taste of the water, let your body sing with this delight, this awakening. Put the ladle back. Lower the bucket. Know that the well is there for you always, with the cool, soothing, refreshing liquid of love.

Suffering for you feels difficult, but it just IS. Once again, proving it is unnecessary. You ask "why" with suffering, "why" it cannot be proven. It IS. Love cannot be proven. It IS. You say, "But I am this or that." You ARE. You feel with each emotion. Look at this, Mary. Examine what I am really saying here: You feel you are with an emotion. You feel you ARE this emotion.

If you feel bad, then you think you are bad. You are this emotion. If you feel good, then you are good. Do you not see how you become your feelings? You wear feelings as if they were clothes. You adopt the total stance of that feeling as if it were you! Do you see that feelings are not trust as it IS? You have been told that you were bad. So you have thought, I AM bad. Don't you see this is NOT who you ARE? You adopted feelings as truth, because you were told so. And you believed. You thought that something was so wrong with you. That you were wrong! Wrong to BE!

The truth was there, and once you fought to believe it. You had to *fight to be believed. But when you are so young, you cannot defend yourself in such a big world. You adopted beliefs. You stopped fighting for self. You became the feeling.*

This is a lot to digest now. I have to think this over. But I thank you, dearest angels and Gracie, for these jewels of thoughts.

I love you, my darlings.

Dearest Angels and Gracie and all that is,   June 20, 1995

Thank you for this day and for my family, for the music and for the cigarettes. Can you please guide me with Amanda and my feelings? I feel all this love for her and then I get scared. When I get scared, I know I appear more rigid than I feel inside. I lost Grace, and I ask myself, *Can I love again? Can I open up to a child?*

Turn toward the light. You have already found what is needed. It is time to clear your mind. You know what is needed. Love who you are and your higher self will be seen. Love will always help you. Clear your mind, Mary.

How can I love myself more?

Go within, and you will be guided. Go inward with a clear mind. You search and want signs. They are all around. Amanda needs to love self. You can teach her this love of self. She struggles as you struggle. Her pain is your pain. But you take this pain on. You become her pain. You blame yourself for her pain. This is her pain. You take on pain that is not yours. Realize this pain is a teacher to indicate what is needed. Remember, what is needed is chosen.

Look at pain, for it is only an indication that will point to love. Love self and go within for these answers. Dip into the well. Take a drink. Your frustrations stem from nonlove. Emptiness. Love yourself and allow this love to guide you. Ask what you can do for self. You use work to get away, to hide from who you are. If you are busy, you do not need to go within. I say to go within. Do not fear. Your strength is great. You know love.

There are those around you who want to show you love. There is healing all around. There are ways. What gives you pleasure, Mary? Examine this closely. Does this also give you love? Do not be afraid to ponder. As you ponder, you will Be. You are wonderful. Celebrate this.

Dearest Angels and Gracie, my love, and all that is, thank you for these insights. I feel calmer. Once again, you are working your magic and LOVE.

My dearest Angels and daughter Gracie,   June 1995
    I am sitting here in the morning, feeling the sun, listening to birds, and sipping coffee. My mornings used to be spent running around and feeling stress. Thank you for helping me to create time where I thought there was none. Thank you for helping me notice my love, my goodness. Thank you for opening my eyes simply to notice.

    I sit here and I think and I wonder. Could you guide me with the issue of having another baby? Some days I desire one, and then I think, *Oh, no, I am fine.* What is going on inside me?

Mary, go inward. You have your answers. Give yourself space. You are creating it now. You are changing your LIFE. SELF is becoming

103

blessed. Your desires are your desires. There is no right and wrong. There Is only being. You want to figure it all out. There is no figuring. Simply Be and trust. You worry constantly. You have spent so much time involved in the future. Just Be in the now.

Think of strength. You are seeing how this carried you through your worst fear. You felt you would crack, not be able to go on, but you did. You believed.

I realize now that I believed in love. Didn't I? I had to hang on to this love, because the pain would only lead to a black hole. This love was like some type of boat in a sea of huge crashing waves. I just clung to the boat in hopes of something.

Yes! In your darkest hour you believed in love. Only love. You ask yourself now, "Would I be patient and responsible with a baby?" Think of what you have just asked. You are patient and responsible now. You work, you listen, you are there for people, you are a true friend. Would it be different with a child? You fear you do not have qualities. That you lack something, somehow, because your daughter died. This is thinking with scarcity. This is thinking that you have some type of drastic deficit. Realize all you do have and are. Say, "I am wonderful."

Know what a good mother you already are. A child can be a reflection of love, of All that Is. Celebrate all that is, all that you are! Take time to love self. We love you also, dear one. Your preciousness is there and we are with you in this awakening.

Dearest Gracie and my angels,   July 8, 1995

I am back on the back porch writing this by hand, and once again I am struck by the beauty of the yard, the flowers, the robins. Thank you for this appreciation, for the ability to notice things that surround me. I keep feeling as if I need to be working on something. Can you guide me? I had another thought of thanks, and that is for Amanda. She was so dear to me today—serving me food and bringing my books to me here on the porch. I feel as if Gracie is working through Amanda.

Amanda's love is Gracie's love. It is all love. There is a connection here—love flows through children. They are pure in so many ways until there is forgetting. Keep these memories alive. Remember love is all there IS. Learn from this love. All is as it should be. Feel. Do not be afraid. Past hurts may come rearing up. You cannot redo, undo, for they are in the past. To cling is not to live in the present. Feel and know silence. All you are reading reflects the pause. This is the place in which you can be. It is between all moments. It is in the timelessness of being. This is needed for good reason. Busyness keeps one away from self.

Working to escape can be difficult for the soul. You tremble at the thought of quiet and knowing. What could you discover that you do not already know? Trust, which is so crucial in life, is there. Remember to Be. The need to control feels troublesome to you. But why? What can you control? Yourself? Others? Reflect on this. You are changing. You are seeing. Dear Mary, you have all the love inside. It is there. Do not be afraid to bring it forth. Love is in the air. Breathe in love. Exhale worry. We are here in your heart. Trust that we will guide you always, should you ask. It is in asking that the knowing is revealed.

I say this often, but love who you are, as you are, now! Know we are there inside this love. To be busy is not always what one needs. Please rest. Feel us within your love.

You tend to work at everything. You continually are working at an improvement for some future goal. What of now? Do you feel as if you are nothing until you get there? Base your thoughts on the internal. Like in between—that is the now. That is The Moment. Let things be. There is no other way to love self than in the now. When you love self, all will fall in place. You will be able to recognize the flow and the integration of self to higher self. You are seeing how one can divide one's self into compartments—integration will come. All this you sense because it will help you. Practice in the moment. Take time for yourself. Know we love you!

Thank you dear angels—Gracie. Mama loves you! I know you are with me.

Dearest Angels and dearest Gracie,   July 1995

I woke up today with questions. Once again I am on the back porch, feeling the sun on my skin. I feel love in my heart for my husband, for Amanda. I feel so blessed. Thank you.

It is true you are at the right place at the right time. Questions are a beginning point, a knowing. To ask questions means the answers are there. Let us speak of perfectionism. Your thoughts recently reflect that you are knowing and seeing that the imperfect is perfect. That one does not have to be perfect as you have been taught to think. Perfection is not joy. Joy is in knowing that imperfection, as you term it, is perfection. This was revealed to you—through Gracie, your daughter. Through physical imperfection of the body, you saw only love.

Yet you struggle. You say, "But I felt I could not care for her." This is your own prison. You create this thought. It has been revealed to you, through Grace's physical problem, that this is not so. Gracie was much more than a body with physical ailments. And you know this to be truth. Gracie came to you, in one sense, to reveal this. Yet you blamed yourself, saying, "But I did not love her enough." That was fear. Do you not see how much you did love her at this time? The angel was there and you felt her presence. Your fear stems from taking care of things—that you do not do it perfectly. It is in the imperfection that there is perfection! Are you worried about your own imperfection? Do you not spend hours needlessly worrying that you have done something wrong? This is a long tradition in your family—one shivers to think of making mistakes, saying something wrong, doing an action differently. That is fear. Believe that you Are. That all you do is perfect in its imperfection.

Gracie blessed you with this. Make mistakes. Celebrate! The goal is to be with all one is, with imperfections. Celebrate your seeing this wonderful condition of humanness. It is through this that joy can be attained and seen.

Notice all around you. This will lead to ultimate forgiveness of self, to integration, to love. I say that in the loving forgiveness, we become whole. It is in the splitting of self—this self is okay, this self is not—that things take on lower vibrations. Vibrate with the knowing. All is well, my dear.

Thank you so much—this is what I need to hear. Yet it scares me, this letting go.

What would happen if you let go? Would you disappear? Lose your mind? Fear again—it is familiar for you. Ask if you fear happiness. Turn inward. Go deep, Mary. Think of Love. The ultimate chuckle is that all is as it should be. Know that! Love will come!

Thank you once again, my dears, and precious Gracie.

Dearest Grace and my Dear Angels,   July 1995

I want to thank you for dear Amanda. So often when I go into this shell, she is there to pull me out. One of the things that touches me so deeply is this dance we do. Grace, we have done this ever since you were alive. . . .

When you were still living, Amanda and I just had to get away. I had hardly spent any time with her, so one day, on the way home from the hospital, we went to listen to CDs at a music store. I remember feeling so lost. I found an old CD from a woman named Angela Bofill. I bought it because it brought back a part of my past, so many years ago. There was a song about an angel on the CD, which we listened to when we got home. We joined hands and began twirling around. We kept going faster and faster. I remember hearing my laugh and thinking it sounded so far away. Grace, it felt so good. What would I do without your dear sister?

Dear Angels,   July 1995

Tonight I feel so tired. I made a mistake at work. I had these booklets printed up with the wrong title. I thought they were proofed, and I was wrong. I feel "bad" now. Please help me! I need to be able to live in the moment and I feel I am always somehow taken out of it.

The now is a strange and wonderful thing. This is not a contest. You are learning. You expect so much so soon. Be, dear one. Be. The more you are able to Be, you will Be. You know, through your mind, that you need to quiet down. Yet you ask yourself why? how?

You feel the warm caress of the breeze. That IS. You see the colors. They Are. Quiet brings internal focus. You are not stuck on the outside of self. Go inward and love. You are so important. Yet, in so many ways, you put yourself last. When I say rest, Rest. Gather. Stroll. Be quiet. What would your life be if you just rested and loved and did not work one weekend? Savor life! Feel it! Be with love. The rest will follow!

Thank you so much my dears! I am so tired I must sleep.

Dearest Gracie,   July 1995

I don't know where to begin with yesterday. I was on the sunporch reading. Your father was out running errands. We have a rule in the family that each of us can ask for "private time" to be alone and uninterrupted. I had told Amanda that I would be taking some private time, but right after I started reading, Amanda knocked at the French doors. I told her again that I was reading, but she said that she had to talk to me. I could tell by the look on her face that something had happened.

She sat on the futon beside me and said that she had gone outside to get some lemonade, when she saw a toddler on the chair I had left outside. At first, Amanda thought it was a neighbor kid, but then she saw white light surrounding the child. I grabbed Amanda's arm; I had goose bumps. I said, "Amanda, who was the child?" Maybe I said it too loud, but Amanda said that it was you,

109

Grace! I asked her how she knew—she said by your curly hair and your eyes. The child then went into this light.

I told Amanda to show me outside. We went outside and Amanda showed me how she had looked under the cushion of the chair after the child disappeared. She said the child had dissolved "into light." Amanda did not know the word for *dissolve*—she just made fluttery motions with her hands. She went on to say that the light was "brighter than the sun."

Gracie, you would have been a year old next week! Amanda said that you had a pink robe on, with stars and moons on your moccasins. Moccasins? She said that there was fur around your robe, and that there was some type of sash that had hearts on the end of it. Gracie, this is almost more than I can bear.

That evening, Amanda wanted to go to the park, so we went. Instead of playing like she usually does, on the monkey bars, she took my hand and told me that Daddy and I should have another child! Gracie, is this from you?

But things don't end there. When I told Julie today at work about what Amanda saw, she told me she had a dream last night in which one moccasin was left at her front door in the rain! Julie has never dreamed about a moccasin before in her life. Gracie, I know you are trying to reach out. I just want to thank you for all of this—but I have to try and figure what it all means. . . .

BELIEVING

July 16, 1995

Dearest Angels, Gracie my love, God—all the universe!

I am sitting on the back steps listening to church bells. I just reread the passages of this journal. It is so wonderful, a blessing, and it helps quiet me. I think of angels and miracles *all* the time. I think of Gracie appearing for Amanda. I ponder the mystery and beauty of life. I realize the pain of Grace's death is turning into a beautiful awareness—a gift of eternity. A revealing of love—a love that knows no bounds. A sense that love is always there. Thank you so for showing me.

I am here and I know instinctively that I might be pregnant. I have felt that I have to take care of my body, that my life is changing. This thought of a new baby makes me feel so hopeful, alive, grateful. Thank you again, my angels.

Yet, there are times when fear crosses my path with this happiness. Can you guide me through this thought?

Dearest Mary,

Fear is fear. It is nothing. Believe in all— All that Is! You saw how fear can control you, yet this is illusion. Illusion appears as fact. Yet there are no facts. Life simply Is.

This is the time for strength and joy! Your strength is in your decision to have another child in spite of fear! You lived your worst fear and came out with more love in your heart. Dear Mary, celebrate life. Know that joy is with you. Feel it. Allow yourself permission to rejoice—welcome love with your family. Know that the time for love is here. Your heart is open. Love yourself and all else follows. Go inward and see. You will be a wonderful mother.

Thank you, Angel, but how can I work with this fear?

To deny anything gives power to what is denied. Accept that this happened. That was then. You are in the now. It is a new experience with all the differences and pleasures of the new. Be gentle. You have already seen that you can turn an argument—whatever it may be—around through love. All of life may be turned around through love. If fear crosses your path, say: "My lesson is learned. I am in a different place, a different time. I am different!" You have nothing to fear. It is only a thought that you choose to think. You can choose to think many things. CHOOSE dear Mary. It is your right! Choose to say, "I am happy."

You have looked fear square in the face and you have found love! Ponder this! You felt fear and grew to love! An immense thing has occurred! You turned something around through love!

Dearest Angels! You wonderful, wonderful beings! You are so helpful. Thank you. And my dearest spirit daughter—you are my precious angel. Thank you!

Dearest Angels, Gracie my darling,   July 23, 1995

Thank you for leading me to the book for parents that have lost their children. It could not have come at a better time than on the eve of Gracie's first birthday. There are so many universal feelings that parents have during this time. I felt as if I were not alone! Thank you.

Yet, I am struck by going back to my grief, anger, bewilderment over Grace's death. I realize I may always have a hole in my heart. I was so upset yesterday, crying and lost. I feel angry. I looked at the outfit Grace would have worn home and the outfit just lay there on the bed—empty.

I sometimes feel as if this was punishment for me—that I did something wrong in this life or a past life. I know death happens to us all. But this seems so hard to deal with and to make sense of—that it happened to a little baby. Can you guide me in making any sense of this? I feel so lost right now. Even as I write, I am somewhere else—jumping up to tell Amanda what to do, talking to John.

There is something in this. Look deeply at these distractions. What is hardest for you to bear? That you have gone back to the place of

113

Grace's death? What are your feelings? Shame, anger, envy? Look inward. Bring the light. You feel doubt right now as to how far you have come. You want things to be happy, not uncomfortable. You want to move on, yet an emotion says wait. Examine why this emotion has made you pause.

Your humanness keeps you back in this place. Yet you realize there is also a place where spirit rests. Dear one, you are only resting for a moment here, in this place of discomfort. You know the depth of your love for Gracie. You judge so harshly. Do not judge. Gracie feels only love for you. Why do you punish yourself for her death? She had a malformation.

Gracie wants you to know she felt all your love, every moment. And what a love it was and still is! You think back and say, "But there were times I wanted her to die—I was not strong enough." Instead, know that you did not want her to suffer—this is love. Your humanness also had concern about her care in the future. This is all right! Gracie felt only your love! Do you not think she sees beyond doubt and despair? These choices that you rivet yourself around were all about love.

This was an extremely difficult, unbearable situation on your physical plane. Know that Gracie knows. She wants you to forgive self. When doubt springs into mind, know Gracie will guide you. She knows how difficult these thoughts and feelings are. Know that they will be replaced with love. Deep, true love.

Dear Grace and my Angel,   August 1995

Your sister, Amanda, and I were at the Bruegger's Bagels restaurant on Grand Avenue last Sunday, when we noticed this older man, kind of a fatherly type, kept looking at us. When Amanda got up to get something, he told me what a beautiful daughter I had. I thanked him and didn't go into the stepdaughter thing, but then he looked me square in the eyes and said that I should have another child! I was somewhat stunned, because I know that I don't look like I'm in my twenties. Amanda just told me to have a child—now a total stranger! Gracie, you know that your father and I have been trying to have another child. But nothing has happened. Maybe I am afraid or something. Yet I found this comment so disarming.

Dearest Angel and Gracie,   August 1995

I am seeing connections everywhere! I have to talk to Margaret and Julie about this tomorrow at work.

Today your father and Amanda and I went to the Minnesota Landscape Arboretum. I thought it would be a good family thing to do. Well, your father and I each had our own agenda of the afternoon. Your dad got a map and I hardly ever read maps, so he was mad at me about this. I thought that we could hike and just be out, and maybe sit in the woods, or a field, or something. But your father wanted to drive everywhere! It was so hot and sticky that everyone started getting crabby. To make a long story short, we ended up in the Japanese garden, then we moved into the shade gardens. I took my little notebook out to write down the names of flowers and plants. While I was doing this, Amanda said that one of her favorite girl's names was Persephone. I tried to ignore this, but I got goose bumps when she said it. Persephone was the daughter of Demeter in Greek mythology, the one that the astrologer had said was in my chart! Well the day went on, and it kept getting hotter. I had to find a place to sit down. Your father and Amanda went out on their own. After I rested, I went to look for them, but I got the directions mixed up.

All of a sudden, I saw this statue by these bushes, so I went over to read the plaque. It was a life-size statue of a man in a loose-fitting garment, with a bird on his hand. It said it was St. Francis of Assisi, the patron saint of small animals and nature, or something like that. Well, I looked over to the side of the statue, and I saw a statue of a German shepherd. Gracie, it was the same one that was in my dream about the burial! It was this magnificent animal. The statue was in the exact position that it had been in my dream, except in my dream, the dog was alive.

I have to ask Margaret about St. Francis. I may even have to stop at a bookstore to get a book on him. Gracie, when I saw that dog statue I almost collapsed. Maybe it was the heat. And the funny thing about this is that no one else was around. It was just me, St. Francis, and his dog.

That night . . .

Dearest Angel and Grace,

This is almost more than I can handle! Tonight Amanda and I were working together, cutting some fabric for a dressing table for her room. As we were doing this, Amanda said again, "It's just like Persephone." I couldn't stand it anymore! I asked Amanda how she knew that name. She said that she had heard it in her "dream of favorite names," and then she added that she'd had that dream last April. She wanted to know why I wanted to know. I told her it was an old Greek name and not many people knew it (let alone a nine-year-old child). That was all that was said. But Grace, it was about last April, actually March 28 to be exact, that all of this started happening, with the computer and all. Have these connections spread to Amanda?

Hello again my Angel and Gracie,   August 1995

Well, this St. Francis story continues. I told Margaret and Julie all about my dream and what I found in the arboretum. They have been having dreams as profound as I feel mine to be. The wonderful thing is that we can share. No one is alone.

After that, Margaret brought in this picture of St. Francis she "happened" to find. I have it by my desk at work. Then, when I was out at my mother's the other day, I was relating the story about the dog in my dream, and the statue at the arboretum. My mother told me that the prayer of St. Francis of Assisi had been my grandmother's favorite prayer! It had been read at her funeral, at which I had given the eulogy. My mother then ran and got the prayer that had hung in my grandmother's bedroom. She gave it to me, as a gift from Grandma.

The interesting aspect of my grandmother is that she was an incredible animal lover. When we were kids, she could not even watch a cowboy movie if horses fell down or were shot. A few days after my grandmother died, two years ago, I had a dream in which I saw her in a white car. I remember she was trying to tell me something, but I could not understand her through the car window. I also remember finding a kitten at a gas station, after planning my grandmother's funeral. I ran to the car with the kitten and showed my mother. My mother ended up keeping this kitten. It was right before John and I were married. It's funny, I never put any of this together before. I'm even beginning to see how animals may be connected to healing . . . and St. Francis is the patron saint of this . . . it's really got me thinking. Thank you, Angels.

August 16, 1995

Dearest God, my Angels, and my wonderful Gracie!

John came home the other day and said, "We have to get another kitten." I was in total agreement with this. I had been thinking how lonely Bob, Amanda's cat, must get when we are at work. Your father does this all the time. It is as if he can read my mind.

We got in the car and headed for Taylors Falls, along the St. Croix River. The animal humane society there is located in a renovated Victorian mansion. I immediately fell in love with the woman who was running it. She took us upstairs and showed us a small orange kitty with golden eyes. The woman gave me the kitten to hold and then said, "She was found on July 22." My heart started pounding. That was your birthday, Grace.

"What?" I said when she told me this. "July 22," she said again. I would not put the kitten down. I told John, "This is the one!" When we were downstairs and John was filling out the papers, I happened to glance at a table and I saw a card that read:

> "Cats are angels with fur,
> Welcome to the tunnel of Love"

Gracie, I knew this to be a sign. First the kitten was found on your birthday. I found it so odd that this woman would even tell us the day that she was found. And then the card. It was all too much. I cried all the way home. Your dad kept looking at me and holding my hand. I kept my fingers in the cat carrier, touching this new kitten. You see, I never took you home, Grace. This was the first thing I could hold in my arms. I just knew that you wanted me to have something to hold. This kitten became christened as Carli. I think she opens up my heart.

Thank you, darling.

August 29, 1995

Dear God, my precious Angels, Gracie my darling,

As you know, I am on the North Shore, sitting on some huge rocks overlooking Lake Superior, hearing the waves crash against the shore. It is a mysterious day, a little dark, almost as if it might rain. John and I have taken some time off to come up here. This was the starting point of our love, years ago, and it continues on, each visit here to these cabins contains a new depth, a new layer to our lives. It is also the perfect place to be on the anniversary of Gracie's death. Even as I write these words it is hard for me.

Mary, look at the water. What does it contain—the beginning of life? The depth you are feeling? The mystery? Reflect. Everything comes forth as it should. Your destiny, your love, your life. You are in the void. What do you see there? What do you feel? It is from this point that answers may be formed. The mystery of life is that it IS! It will always be! Acceptance is crucial now. To love All includes love of self. Savor the furry spiders of your dreams. For they are only furry pets! They are nothing to fear! Your fear has controlled you—almost stopped you, deadened you from movement. But in the void, you can walk and touch this fear. Hold it near love. It is only by love that life will be transformed. You are in exactly the right place on this trip. To add a new layer of love! To visit the void, to gain strength! You had strength for Gracie. Now it is time to have it for yourself. Everything that you were for your daughter still lies within you. This time, this day that you have been waiting for, is here, and it is from this time that the new beginning can occur.

Thank you, my angels and Gracie. I love you, too.

Dearest Angels, Gracie, and God,   September 1995

I am sitting outside. The summer is almost over. The breeze is blowing. I keep sensing something about "illusion." I know I should look it up.

Illusion is set up to teach, to break through to the light and love. When illusions are cast aside, one can see.

Do you think I need to let go of my illusions? Do I have illusions in my life?

You thought today of illusions; therefore, you questioned. But you also heard. You cannot see illusions, yet one knows the difference when one is on the other side of illusion. There is no illusion. There is only fear set up to deceive. Yet what is fear but what one thinks is so? Nothing is meant to harm you. Nothing. The illusion is a trick, a sleight of hand in perception. Nothing more. Go to the quiet. Love is there! You worry so about this and that, about tricks, about mistrust. Be still. Be quiet. The answers are there.

I feel as if I have trusted and I have been tricked in love. I have believed and then I have been hurt! What does this mean? Was this not done to me? Against me? What do I need to learn?

Mary, you have made your heart like armor for protection—in many ways with good cause. It is difficult to convey on your terms what choice means, that you have chosen certain paths to learn from. Reflect on your life. Have you chosen pain?

Does anyone choose pain?

The picture of life is much bigger than how you are examining it. The stage for your life was set a long time ago. You chose, yet your journey is what you are remembering—the pain of the journey. My dear one, has not this journey taught you, deepened your perceptions of life, stretched your imagination to the wonders? Do you not see that with

*each painful lesson, you have reaped benefits far greater than what you
cried over at the time of pain? Your divorce propelled you to know what
true love meant and is. Hence, John. Your marriage to John is a symbol
of your happiness, your choice even through pain! The life and death of
Gracie have brought you toward spiritual transformation. This pain that
humans try so hard to understand is merely a lesson of choice. But this
choice is hard to fathom.*

*Yes, you are on the brink of letting go of illusions, but part of you
clings to the familiar. What awaits is true happiness. Joy! Trust in this
movement toward joy! There is never too much. When perplexed, when
filled with insecurities, go to the quiet. Know your answers are there.
Do not be afraid of what you try so hard to deny. You are on the road to
Joy and Joy awaits you with open arms.*

*You want to do it all so right, so correctly. Just be! Have you not
thought that by acceptance a major lesson has been accomplished?
Listen to your inner voice, the voice that IS. If something is nonsupport-
ive, hard, difficult, berating, it is fear! Do not worry about outcomes.
Just be. Take time and enjoy.*

Oh, my angels, with all of your help, I will learn to simply be and accept. Thank you. I love you all.

Dearest Angel and Grace,   September 1995

I have to come to you once again. I feel as if I do not
understand. I have tried to get into my computer—I
can't count the times, and all I get are those bells. I can't
write with it. Once again I am not complaining, but this is
unnerving. As much as I see all these wonderful things,
all these connections, I still have this fear. And I still cry

at night so much. Not as much as when you first died, Grace, but every time I think of your being gone, I start crying privately in my pillow. I just stare out into this dark room and wonder about everything. *How could this have happened to me?* How come I still wonder and have fear? And why won't the computer work?

BEING

Dearest Angels, my God, darling Gracie,

Today, Amanda came back home from her other house, and I was a mother again. It feels so good when she and I set up our rhythm—our way of being. I really love her. I love being a mother. It means so much to me. Thank you for this in my life.

You have come to this point in your life because you have chosen it. What Amanda reveals to you is a reflection of yourself, the self you need to love. As you see and admire parts of her, are intrigued by parts

of her, and are repelled by other parts, know that you do this with self.
You are who you are. You are Mary, as Amanda is Amanda.

And now you question. You are seeing connections for the first time!
You are being. You look at the measure of your thoughts. You are ques-
tioning: Is this thought right for me? You are solving the riddle of love,
of acceptance, of knowing.

Mary, dear, you are trusting. As you have thought, you are treating
this writing, this journal, as valid. You come here to know. You realize
that by holding this journal, it is real, concrete. These are so much more
than words. You see the truth within the words.

Do you not feel your joy? Open your arms, my dear! You believe
these words, and in so doing love yourself! The miracles are soon to be.
We love you. We shall always be close.

September 22, 1995

Dearest Angels, Gracie, and the Wonderful,
Beautiful Universe!

Today I am sitting at a cabin with Julie and Margaret.
We are here on a retreat. We have wanted to spend time
together, away from homes and families. These women
are so special and giving. We each have struggled, and
may continue to struggle, but the support and love we
feel for each other is wonderfully loyal and poignant at
the same time. Yet, as I drove here, I felt anxious or
excited or something. Can you shed some light on this?
Can you help me?

There is a connection here, a knowing. Where does this lead? Anxiety

125

and excitement. It is a discovery, a new road, the point at which you all come together. This love is so revealing. Let go at this moment and blow the past away as dust on your fingers. For it is done. This moment, this time, is the beginning of the new, and from this—through this—love springs forward like a babbling brook catching the sun. Imagine the life! The vitality! The love! As you turn from pain, you can feel the transformation. This will replace the pain. Your love is like a jewel to be examined on all sides.

Thank you so much for this space and time, for this insight, for this love, my angels. Thank you.

Later that day . . .

Dear angels,

Today the most incredible event happened to me. Next to seeing the scrolling computer, this has to be the strongest visual thing I have ever witnessed. . . .

Because Margaret and Julie and I did not know what we were going to be doing at the cabin, we just let things go on their own. We talked and ate bread and cheese. We played music. We said the prayer from Grace's funeral service. We burned candles and laughed and cried. We were just women together.

At one point, the three of us were sitting on the living-room floor. I happened to look over at Julie. As I did, I saw a shaft of light come through the living-room ceiling. It was light blue and had white iridescent bubbles in it. The aspect of the light that was so very striking was that it was moving. As if it were alive! The bubbles moved within the light. At this moment I knew and felt that time had totally stopped. It was the most beautiful light I have ever seen. I can only attribute this to you, Grace. This light was completely without fear. It was simply beautiful.

Dearest Angels and Gracie,   September 26, 1995

I dreamed last night that I was running down a hallway at work. My job had moved. I entered what I knew to be the "Zeus Room," because I saw this picture of Zeus on the wall. I saw a table with a puzzle on it. The puzzle had intricate and tiny pieces. I started to pick up one of the pieces, but decided it would upset the whole puzzle, so I left it alone. Angels, when I think of this, I see how perplexed I am with my life, how the pieces don't seem to fit. Is it better left alone, or do I need to figure something out? Yet, I cannot help but be comforted by these dreams.

I sit here now, on a warm autumn day. I hear the birds, feel the sun, see the bumble bee on a flower, and I want this moment to last. This beauty that surrounds me, this way of nature seems so perfect. It all fits. One season blending into another. Change and harmony. Can we talk of my destiny? My purpose? Does it have anything to do with beauty?

You sense and you know. All of your life has been about beauty. But what is beauty but a reflection, a reflection of who you are? You have worked so hard at making things beautiful on the outside that you have hungered for beauty on the inside. But you knew. You see so much. And with this seeing is the need to transform, to touch something and bring out its beauty. This all springs from your inner beauty. You see, you touch, you transform—all because of your inner beauty. Everything in your life has centered on beauty—your clothing, your home, your food, your life.

But it is only now that you know this. Beauty, like all else, can hold a duality, a lesson. Beauty for the sake of externals can lead to emptiness, hollowness—just as love can be hollow if there is no self-love. You have passed through these gates in search of beauty. You pushed beauty to the limits, to mold a perfectionist attitude that imprisoned. But this is not inner beauty. This is what you have always sensed—always known.

This perfectionism became evident in Grace with her malformation. Your biggest fear was that your child would not be "perfect." That you were not perfect! Yet, you truly saw that Grace was perfect just as she was in physical form. Your heart held the truth through LOVE. And nothing matters now but love. Your "imperfection" is your perfection.

Beauty has taken you down many roads, from the physical to the celestial. And yes, this knowing of beauty is magical, transformational. When you understand this beauty, you will be free!

How can I use this beauty for the highest good?

You have knowledge. You know that human perfection on your plane is impossible. To strive for this leads to emptiness, to loss. What do you give away to reach this goal? Your heart! This is what spirituality all points to. It is accessing What Is! What will always Be!

You have known the brittleness of beauty with no heart. Yet you sense this knowing, this teaching to reach beauty—inner beauty. Feel the feeling of looking at a beautiful flower or seeing a curtain blow in the breeze. What happens to you? This is what we speak of.

As you reflect on beauty totally in the moment, you are present. You know perfection. You know that everything contains beauty—even pain. Dear one, this road you have traveled has held its arms open to you. And you have embraced it! Do you not feel a lightening of spirit?

I keep sensing that I have seen this beauty in others but not in myself. That I know beauty, although it seems distant. . . .

You know! You know beauty in others—you bring out the beauty in others because you see their beauty! You reflect this back to others. When others have walked the road of pain, you have seen their beauty! You have reflected this back to others. Do you not see that the beauty you saw in others was your own beauty reflected back? And what beauty! What love! Through pain you saw beauty in others! Celebrate this awakening! Your beauty is bountiful!

I feel my spirit is lighter, happier, knowing the beauty has always been in me! And I never knew until now. I didn't realize how beautiful I was. Oh, thank you, dear angels! My God! I love you so! Gracie darling! What an angel you are. I will celebrate my beauty.

September 30, 1995

Dearest Angels, my daughter Gracie, God,
and the Wonderful Universe,

I am in bed now on a Saturday night. All is quiet in the house. I have reflected on the name Bridge for my Guardian Angel. This sense has been with me since I first wrote. Am I on to something?

You are Mary, and it Is. Bridge. A connection from one side to the next. A means of traveling, communicating.

Is it okay that I call you that?

What stops you?

I am afraid.

Why?

Afraid that I named you. That you already have a name— that Margaret said you were Trinity. I know you are with me but I have not felt any communication coming through—as if there were silence. I wonder if you are mad.

Are you sure you are not angry? At yourself? You worry about being who you truly are. So you seek approval from outside, even when you have answers. Why do you do this? Why do you torture self and set self up for defeat? You know. Act on this. You don't need my approval to be who you are and to feel how you feel. Be, dear one! We speak now of responsibility to self. This is essential to trust. One must trust self, and to do so, one must be responsible to self.

Thank you for this insight. I am still in a quandary about your name. I feel somewhat insecure in this regard. The act of naming anything just seems so important. I guess if Margaret heard "Trinity," I'll go with that. I hope this will be okay with you. Perhaps bridge was the symbol for you, my angel.

BEING

Dearest Angels, Trinity, my Gracie, dearest God,
and the Wonderful Universe,

I just want to thank all of you for the love and kindness you are sending me—the insights and illuminations. I feel as if I am growing and understanding more each day. I just want to be! Yet as I pause here, I think of my frustration today. My needing to get things done, my not being pregnant. I felt edgy. Then I get snappy and controlling.

You want to control what you cannot. This has been evident to you. Think of the pause and what it contains. There is a reason for the pause—a most important function. The richness and depth are within. Be ever so gentle with self. All will get done! Sort—see what can be discarded and what contains your true essence. Realize your beauty! Be gentle.

The pause is the most important moment you will experience. It is in the unexpected poignant moments with your child, petting an animal, allowing life to unfold within. Control defeats the purpose of this. The riches come from within, from noticing, from being present. Don't "do" anything. Try being, giving your all to the moment! Then you will see. You will treasure being Mary!

Think of your happiest times. Were they not the sunset? the music? the fire? the unexpected pleasures of love? the realness of spoken truth? Be real! This concept of being genuine Is. This will help you touch what you search for. The more you love yourself, the more we are able to help you.

Thank you my beings of light and love, my darling Grace. I love you all. Thank you so.

October 5, 1995

Dearest Angels, Gracie my Light,
the Wonderful Universe,

I guess I didn't get too angry with Amanda this morning—she was running late for school again. Yet, I am still left with a residue of feelings, of feeling unsettled—bad somehow.

Look at this word—bad. What does it signify to you?

I feel as if I am bad because I have these feelings.

Feelings are not bad or good. They simply are. In the transparent state they can enter and leave. Send yourself love on these occasions. Work from the internal out. Go to the quiet when you feel these feelings that are not favorable. As you go inward, you will understand. Love is there. But it starts with self. You are thinking of authenticity. Start with your emotions. Do you accept them or do you push them away when they arise?

You want the feeling of love in these situations, yet you show no love to self! If you are sad or angry, shake hands with this emotion, send it love. It is at this point that you turn on self. You punish self for being human, and therefore you punish others. This love of self is paramount. Start here.

Do you always have to wait until you feel positive emotions before you love self? Integration takes time. Start by loving you! Celebrate by loving you. You looked fear in the face. How about anger? Hold its hand and by doing so learn to love.

Thank you, Dear Angels and Gracie and the Universe.

October 17, 1995

Dearest Trinity, Gracie my love, my dearest Angels, dearest God, and all the Wonderful Universe,

It has been so long since I last wrote. As you know, I have been to New Orleans for a work convention. I will soon be off to Spain for the International Symposium.

I did feel more personal power in New Orleans. I know that I am able to connect with people effectively. I know that I do a good job. I feel so happy at times and then angry. I feel I have so much in so many ways. Why do I feel so upset now? Is it because I am not pregnant?

Mary, listen to your heart. It will guide you. Go to the quiet. You wonder about answers. They are there. What bothers you is a reflection of self. Pause in this moment. Call on us. We are there for you.

Remember, when you are troubled to go to the quiet. What are you afraid of? What you will see? What you are? Your beauty? Your love? All are there. Yet you hide—as if this were not your right. Know love is there. We are there. You search for all outside of self. Yet it is all within you. Do not let the externals fool you! Give yourself time daily to be, Mary.

Why am I so sad?

You are sad because you have chosen this. Is it sadness for what is or what could have been? Certainly, when you look at what Is, there is no sadness. You look at the past. Look at the now, the present. Within the present is a present—you! Unwrap this gift.

133

When you love something, what do you love most? What is perfect? Or is it the crooked smile, a little shuffle in the gait of someone you love? Is it not the moment of imperfection that cements—endears you to that person for life? Is it not slipping and falling and being picked up by someone you love that cements the trust within for that person? Is it not the tears and fears that you share with someone that open your heart and bridge you to that person? Is it not the flaws, the very flaws you condemn yourself for, that promote love for others in your eyes?

Give that to yourself. This sadness is yours to hold for the moment. So be it and it will pass. Do you not see that when you are—fully—sadness has no need to stay. You have denied your emotion. It was only waving its hand and stating, "I am here!" Now that you have said hello, it can go!

Mary, when you allow yourself to feel, the feeling passes. When you do not allow the feeling, it stays until you do see it! Treasure this humanness.

Thank you dearest Trinity, Gracie, Angels—thank you—

Dearest Trinity,   October 1995

Trinity, this really is for you, dear Angel. It is you that I want to address. I have been speaking to you, well, since last June. And I have to tell you that it means the world to me. At first, I wasn't aware of the impact of it all. But then I began to reread all our conversations and I began to learn from what had been written. It is as if there is a tailor-made way of looking at my life—of being able to see my life and see it with some type of balance and harmony. You give me that, dear Angel. It is almost as if you are

correcting my thinking, getting me to see through different eyes. And even more than that, I have come to believe
that the words you use have power within them, some
type of healing agent that enters me. Otherwise, how
could I feel this calm—even in the midst of this chaos I
sometimes find myself in? How could that be? I think of
the phrase "just BE." How many times have you told me
that? But maybe if I hear it enough, its power will affect
me and affect my perception. I know this—because even
during periods of fear, I can feel some release when I
speak with you.

Trinity, I will take anything. I want you to know the
gratefulness of my heart for even one minute of your
soothing voice.

November 7, 1995

Hello there, you Wonderful Angels, Dear God,
and the Universe!

Guess what? I am feeling better! I voiced my emotions
to John and my mother, saw my role in things—how my
upcoming birthday and not having a baby and my getting
older all were getting to me. I started feeling closer to
myself, as if there was a place, a time, to forgive and to
love my anger, my emptiness. And love truly does bind
and heal. I know in the big picture, I am learning, but at
the moment it can get difficult. Yet, I wonder, how I can
live with this duality and strive for oneness. I realize med-
itation, just being, is part of all this. But sometimes I work

so hard at trying to get closer to God, to oneness, that I get frustrated. I know I should not try, but I do.

You do try. Let it be. You quickly jump to conclusions, to specifics. This is all part of it! These are your lessons. Let it be! Do not force things. Already you have learned much about self. Integration takes time. You sense that you have to "put this together." This is integration. It will happen. Trust, dear one.

Watch as the tide turns. As you see. Marvel at this stage. Treasure who you are. Time is put on the physical plane to promote sequence. Things do not happen all at once as in thought (inspiration). Time heals and cures. Marvel at this lesson of patience. Patience is your friend. Patience has come to say hello, to slow you down. Savor this.

Thank you for helping me see, to look with gratitude at what I do have. I know you know what is right for me. I will learn (notice I took *try* out of *will learn*). I think it is being in the pause that I must *savor,* for I am here for a reason. Even if I pause with anger, I can hold this emotion and send it love. We can become one together. I can do this with all the dear sides of my being human.

Thank you dearest ones, my Dearest God, and, as always, my Sunshine Daughter, my light beam, *my* wonder—Gracie Darling—thank you!

III.
CONNECTING

BALANCE

Dearest Angels, Trinity, Gracie, Dearest God,
and the Universe,

It is Sunday and John is in bed already. It is only 6 P.M.! I
had time yesterday to rest and read. Thank you, Gracie
darling, for leading me to the books. Thank you for the
curtains I got for the house. The light streaming in the
windows is so beautiful. Every time I see beauty, I feel
love. I love this house so very much. I love John and
Amanda so, so much. My life was empty without them.
Thank you for bringing them into my life.

Yet John and I had a fight (I should say *I* had a fight with John) about doing the laundry—twice he rewashed clothes that had already been washed. I became so upset. What is it with me? Why do I do that? Why do I react so strongly over something so insignificant? Can you help me?

Yes, Mary—I am here to help. You ask why? Why do you think? You are restless. You question work and, more important, what to do with work. What to do with time. What to do with balance.

You want balance and harmony. Yet an outbreak such as this upsets the balance. Why is this? What is to be learned? Think of the process. You have time, therefore, how shall you fill it? By doing, by being, by fighting, you choose. Remember, you choose. But why choose a fight? You choose because it is known from long ago. Yet, the concept here stems from doing, working. Are you angry at self for working or not working? This loss of control makes you wonder what is happening. Your productive, working self is confused by the new rules—the rules of being. It feels lost. Embrace this side of yourself. All is not lost—just be!

Love all sides. This argument was a reflection of your inside. Love who you are at the moment. John can take care of himself.

Thank you my dear ones. I love you all so much.

November 20, 1995

Dearest Trinity, Gracie, and all the Angels,

I started feeling better today toward the end of work. A calm came over me. I felt I had all this time. Thank you. It's as if my days have opened up with time. I don't know why, but I am getting my work done quicker. I'm trying to be authentic, true to myself. Thank you for this insight.

You know I had that fight with John tonight. I wanted to pay bills and he didn't know where they were. It escalated until, well, you know. I felt awful after this fight. My energy was so sapped. Another outburst. I feel I really need help with this part of my integration. If you think this is for the higher good, and that help is what would be for the best, could you help?

Love is there, Mary. In your heart. Think of how you feel during an "outburst," as you put it. Confused, angry, threatened? These are triggers, clues for you. To protect yourself in the past you have fought. As you reflect on your life, know that the justice you have sought has only been the justice you wanted internally.

What is it that you really want at those moments? Love? Give love and you will receive love. It is difficult when things appear unfair. Leave if you must—go to the quiet.

This is a misunderstanding, this conflict. Treat it as such—you misunderstand, you miss understanding the situation. You keep wanting to know if this is a reflection of your inner sides. Yes! Something is misunderstood. That creates conflict. Look into your heart. These interludes are there for a very good reason. You pause and see the lesson! Do you not see that you are seeing? Caress the part of you that needs understanding. The conflicts with John will cease. I promise! Dear Mary, realize that this way of being has been known for a long time. It is a protection. You tremble at change. Yet, on the other side is Joy waiting with open arms. Please be gentle first with your sides, all the aspects of you. It is from this point of gentleness that you will know how to treat others! Breathe in gentleness. Exhale pain! We love you!

I will practice being gentle with myself—I mean my selves, all my dear sides. That poor threatened side needs my love. I think it may be my heart.

You are right! Love your heart. The rest will take care of itself!

November 29, 1995

Dearest Angels, my Trinity, my loving daughter,
the Wonderful Universe,

I had my birthday and it was very special. Amanda, John, and I sang together that night. John recorded our singing. It was wonderful. Yes, there is music coming back into our lives. We also put up our tree and it feels like Christmas. Amanda and I have been wrapping gifts.

I'm having a hard time loving myself. I'm comparing, angry, sad, tired, sick. My emotions seem to fluctuate. I am happy one moment, sad the next. I guess I'm upset because I am not more whole or together. What does this mean? Only if you feel I should know—if you think it is for the higher good.

You have reflected on your shoulders recently. How bowed and droopy they have become. This is weight, the weight of worry, the not knowing, the burdens of life. You have carried so much extra weight. And now it is time to discard your burdens! You fluctuate between two worlds. Make your burdens lighter. Give them up! Just say, "I give you up!" Up to the heavens! I will take your troubles. Now! I will take your sad-

142

ness. Now! I will take your fear. Now!

Replace these burdens with love, light, and joy! Know this surrendering will last forever. There is no need to carry more. Enjoy your family. Enjoy! As of this moment, you are done with pain. Know this, dear one. Feel this within. Your pain has flown on wings to the highest peak. Love remains. Love shadowed this pain you chose. Believe this is gone—this pain. It has taken wings and flown away. Love remains. Feel lighter!

Thank you DEAR ONES! Thank you.

Look at yourself as convalescing. Healing. Give yourself time to heal!

Dearest Angels, Gracie, and Trinity,   December 1995

Work has felt so fragmented lately—we have all been traveling. My world just has not been right until recently, when Margaret got home from Italy. Julie had gotten back from Europe shortly after I did, and we could catch up on things, but I kept watching the days on the calendar. Julie, too, kept asking, "When is Margaret getting back?"

Now she is here, and we can all be together. All three of us have felt such gratitude, just in being with our families. Margaret called me today and wanted me to stop by before work, for coffee. We live only five minutes from each other. Her house was decorated for Christmas. It looked so beautiful.

We sat at her kitchen table, both of us had our dream journals, and we read from them. We both kept smiling. I couldn't help it, I just blurted out how much I had missed her.

I watched her move around the kitchen, getting me coffee, sitting down, and looking at me, and I did not want to leave. I knew how special this moment was.

I just feel so complete with her. It is as if where there are gaps in me, Margaret fills them. I come home when I am with her. That is how it feels. Just like being home.

December 4, 1995

Good morning my dearest Angels and Gracie my love,

Well, I am taking the day off from work. It is a gray day. It looks as if it may snow more. I do like the winter. I like the change of seasons. Is there anything you would like to tell me?

You are pensive regarding change, and it is so—change is on the horizon. Let it be, for it will come. You have asked for this change, and so it shall be. Dear one, you have come far. Please relax! Let us handle the details. You are not used to allowing others to do for you. If I can hold your hand gently and lead you, this will be so. You do not have to work for anything. Your fear has gone—flown!

You move within this new realm as if you were a stranger in a foreign land. The land of allowing. For you have worked hard for this. Yet all one must do is believe. We are in your thoughts. We are part of you. Savor our love for you.

I do feel a shift, a major shift in my perceptions. I'm not waking up angry. I feel as if I do believe and everything is possible!

Yes! Yes! Yes! You are treating your dream life with equal importance to your waking life. You see! You are moved by beauty! Celebrate the beauty of the soul! Love has called and you have heeded it.

Thank you my angels and Gracie darling.

ASKING

December 10, 1995

Dearest Angels, Trinity, my darling Gracie,

We arrived home from Madison tonight. Every year we go to John's parents around Christmas. John's family is so warm. Nancy, his mother, always makes sure that there are activities planned for all of us. I've always admired that she takes such good care of herself. She even told me that I could take a nap if I wanted. It was the middle of the day!

Gracie, I know you are with us in spirit. But as you know, sometimes I long for you so . . . thank you for your

146

love. Amanda is such a great kid. Thank you for helping and guiding her.

Trinity, you know I have been thinking of Margaret, for Margaret. We have grown so close. I feel as if we are traveling together now. She asked for guidance of any type. Can you help? She wonders about her writing and what to do next with it. Please shed light on this if you can, but only for the higher good.

Do not force this; let this flow, for this is an honor. You have crossed this bridge through love. Only love. Feel lighter! You close your eyes and see green, the color of healing, of love. Breathe in and know Love is there. Your heart beats and you feel Margaret's energy. For you are both now connected in this realm.

This connection is of value, you both have traveled far, very far, together and now you are bound by love. As Margaret has lit your path, you too shall light hers. You show one another the way. If one falls, the other is there to console. You are bound by love. Your hearts beat together. You travel together. Your dreams are significant. Let the unfolding take place, for this can only happen with trust. This trust has developed through love.

You speak of unfolding. Does this mean with her writing?

Yes. Her writing will unfold as a flower does. You will see. You will be there. Go to your dreams. You SEE. You know. Margaret looks too hard at what already is in front of her—around her, within her. Look to your dreams. This is not difficult. It unfolds, as a flower does.

Patience is a friend during this time, especially for Margaret. It is there. Trust in this. BELIEVE. This trust is paramount. As you see you share, all of you do, this unfolds. The story unfolds. You trust, you share, you grow. This is life. This is what dreams are made of. This is LOVE!

Thank you my dear ones. Thank you. I will show this to Margaret tomorrow.

December 14, 1995

Dear Angels, dearest Trinity, and Gracie,

I am worried, if I might say, about talking to you, Trinity, for Margaret. Is what I tell her accurate? What if I got something mixed up in the message?

You worry and therefore it is. Do not worry! Do not do this to yourself! Be! Strengthen this tie, this bond. Allow this to happen. What holds you back?

I think of my back—it has been aching this morning. Aching from worry!

Do not do this to self. It is wasted energy. Second guessing. It puts you in a place of never knowing, never being right. Always deficient— scarcity once again. When you make a decision, realize you can change your mind, and then that is it. That becomes your decision. If you change your mind again—then that becomes your decision. You divide self with worry. Go deep within. Let the waves of love surround you. Nurture yourself. Let things be. Love for love's sake only. Caress those parts of you that tend to wander off—just as they are now. Know this is all of you. Don't make yourself right or wrong. Just be! We love you and are with you always.　　　　　　　　　*Lovingly ⇌ The Angels*

Thank you my dear ones.

Dear Universe, Trinity, my Angels, Gracie, my love,

My car was acting up before work today. I ended up walking home because it stalled a couple blocks away. I am grateful for this time. I tried to meditate but I could not silence my mind. I am feeling bad, somehow, again. I am so tired of this feeling, of waking up and feeling bad. Please help me to understand. I feel as if I am trying to make myself wrong. If you think this is for the higher good. . . .

Do not feel there is somewhere you have to be. You are fine just as you are now. You want knowledge, to be at a certain point by a certain time. When I say go deep, go deep! Know this is where your answers lie. Do not fear, Mary. Just be! The present is a present you give yourself. In the stillness, you will find what you are seeking.

Why is it that last week I was so full of the Christmas spirit and now I feel so sad? Why have these feelings come over me? Where does all sadness spring from? Not caring, not having, not being?

Mary, all these sides are a part of you. Do not alienate them and push them asunder. They are gifts of humanness. Treasures. One does not cut one's arm off over a mere splinter. You work with the splinter, soften it, clean the area, ease it out. Or it will work its way out. Love your presence. Cherish these moments.

Your sadness is an ally. It brings you peace and comfort even in distressing times. It says, "I am." Do not judge this emotion. Do you not feel your sense of lightness with no judgment? It is! As with all emotion. Do not rate these feelings and thoughts. They are. Yes, Mary, gentleness is needed! With all emotion!

Thank you dearest Angels, Trinity, and Gracie. I love you.

December 25, 1995

Dearest Trinity, Gracie, my sweet Angels, dearest Universe, dearest God, and Jesus,

Happy birthday, dear Jesus! I never thought that I would ever write a letter to the Son of God, but here goes. And I'm not even religious!

I sit here in the quiet of the morning. Your day, Christmas Day, and I feel love and happiness.

I love John, Amanda, Carli, Bob, my house, my life. I have so very much. As I contemplate the mystery of life, I see how my dearest friends bless my life with their love. Margaret is working on a new book, the story of what the three of us—herself, Julie, and I—have been through as friends. Thank you for all the insights and love; the trust is strong and good and such a wonderful flow.

It is nearing a year since I started writing in this journal. It has been a year of grief, shakiness, learning to live, but, most of all, of love. Trinity, as you speak to me, through me, are with me, you have opened up worlds, depths, layers. You have shown me how I can open up. You stand by me no matter what I experience, and I love you for that, that your love spans over time, without judgment, always pointing the way. You have influenced my life in such positive ways. A kiss and hug for you!

Darling Gracie, you know what you have done for me. You came into my life, a jewel of love. I cry as I write this.

You were so brave, every step of the way. Without you, dearest, I would not be at this point. I will love you for eternity; I will do anything for you. You are my Angel, my highest star, darling! When we meet again, it will be so joyous. I hold you in my thoughts always. . . .

My other Angels, I know you are with me—guiding me, beside me, in my thoughts, my dreams. Although sometimes I don't understand or get the message, know that I want to. I get a little scared or confused if I don't understand. Please bear with me, dearest Beings of Light. I may be a tough case but no one wants to understand more than I. With your Love, I can do it! I love all of you! MERRY CHRISTMAS!

Dearest God, dearest Jesus, I know there is an eternal plan. The vastness of all of this overwhelms me at times. You and only You bring light into my life. Your angels have been wonderful this year (or I have noticed them more!). Thank you for loving me always. Please help me to evolve and move toward you, keeping you in my heart always. May I learn what I can give to humanity in love. Dear God, thank you from the bottom of my heart! I love you!   In Peace and Joy, ∾ Your loving Mary

Dearest Trinity, my Angels, Gracie,   December 27, 1995

I write today because my heart is troubled. Amanda told everyone at work that her mother, John's ex-wife, has written a story about Grace. I felt so bad—it seems so unfair. She was my daughter. Please help me! This troubles me so. . . .

This story must be told, should be told. This story of humanness, of love. You say "my daughter," and yet you care for another woman's daughter. This is a story, and you are Grace's mother. No one can take that away from you. Know this! What Amanda's mother does, she does. You are Gracie's mother and always will be! You feel robbed, but what you cry over is that Grace is not with you in human form. This is the feeling you are picking up, that this was yours and it was taken from you.

Yet, dear Mary, this is every mother's fear—there is no greater pain than the loss of a child. You are all mothers, your friends, your spirit sisters. You walk together on the same path—with love, only love, for your children.

Do not fault yourself for these feelings, dear one. They are. But know that Gracie was born to you, only you, and this love is every woman's story. The bond between you and Gracie knows no place or time. You know this. You have lived this. You could not be writing books as you grieved the loss of Grace—you grieved, and through this your story grew. Know this is your story, your life, but that it belongs to all who touch it. Thank you for turning to me in times of need. May your heart be filled with peace.

Lovingly, ⌒The Angels

Thank you again for your tenderness.

December 27, 1995

Dearest Trinity, my dearest Angels, and as always, darling Gracie,

Margaret just called. I think she is worried about me. She said some pretty amazing things, loving things, at a time when I really needed to hear them. Her dear Angel, Peace, told her to tell me. Thank you for this. She told me her heart was peaceful, or that she was in a peaceful place, and could share it. These are your words to me today, "May your heart be filled with Peace." Yes! I do want peace in my heart, and love! Wonderful love! It is so simple, yet so hard. But it doesn't have to be, does it? I can choose love. I will choose love, only love! Her kindness touched my heart.

Please, dearest Angels, help me to let go and open up to love, if you feel it is for the higher good. I believe in you all so much. And I really, really need you all! Thank you for your love and guidance.

January 4, 1996

Dearest Grace, Trinity, and the Angels
and the Holy Spirit,

Gracie, as you know, I have been writing to you and Trinity for almost ten months by hand. Yet, as much as this has been working, I cannot help but wonder why this computer still will not operate. I have tried and tried to write with it. It has unnerved me more than you know. This has been since it first scrolled that one night. I hear the bells when I turn it on, and I get so rattled. I keep blaming myself for not understanding something. But how can a person understand this?

I ask you Grace, if you could do anything to help. I don't know if you know or anyone knows how upsetting this is to me. I pray that you can help me . . . please help me. I will ask you again in my prayers tonight.

Dearest Gracie,   January 5, 1996

I had to write as soon as I got up this morning. Gracie, I am going to trust in this dream of last night. My heart is just pounding again.

When I woke up, I had the feeling that all was well with the computer. I had a very simple dream last night, but one which I will never forget. I was above a map, an old antique scrolled map. I was looking down at the map when I saw a clipper ship. I knew this to be my ship. It was at a halfway point, heading for some land. I kept squinting from above, trying to see what this land was called. Finally I saw the name. It was called Grace. I knew this to be Graceland. The dream scene switched immediately, from that point. I saw a computer cable, and I knew instinctively that this was my connection to you, Grace.

Grace, I am beginning to look so deeply at my dreams, so very deeply. If you heard me, and this dream really means what I think it does, this alone seems prophetic.

Darling Grace,   January 7, 1996

Two days ago I turned the computer on and wrote my first words. I cannot tell you how relieved I was. I guess I was afraid to trust the dream at first. The signal bells go off when I type certain words, but I can write! I thank you so very, very much, Gracie! I cannot put words to how I feel. I told Margaret and Julie that I had been able to go in and write on the computer. It is the first time in ten months! Julie got tears in her eyes.

I thank you also, dear Trinity. Thank you so very much.

Dearest Grace and Trinity,   January 1996

When I went into the computer just recently to write to you, Grace, I wrote, "Can I †ell you how proud I am of you," because of my being able to write again in the computer. The *t* in *tell* printed as a cross. Now for three weeks, I have been seeing these crosses pop up every now and then in the writing. The bells still go off, but not as much. It appears that the bells emphasize certain words. This is comforting to me, because it makes me think that this connection to you is very right.

Dearest Gracie,   January 1996

I was in my cubicle, working on something this morning, when I turned around to see Margaret. We were the only ones in the office. She had these papers in her hand and her eyes seemed all watery. I still did not know what was going on. She then told me that she had read these letters to you, Grace.

I had given her the letters to look at, because we are working on this book of our experiences together, the three of us—Julie, Margaret, and me. No one has ever seen these letters, because I have been afraid to show them to anyone. Margaret put her arms around me, and I heard her say, "I never knew, I never knew." I felt her compassion for me, and I let it wash over me, Grace.

I felt, Gracie, that a dam of tears was inside of me, waiting for this moment of safety. All the shame I felt just broke when Margaret touched me. It was the first moment that anyone really knew me, for what I was.

It was the first time that anyone ever saw inside my heart.

RECEIVING

Dearest Trinity, Gracie, My Angels,　　　　January 18, 1996

I have come here to understand what is happening to me. I feel sad, as if I have to let go of having a baby. I know I sound like a broken record. John and I are distant. What is happening?

You have a need now to be quiet. So be quiet. This is perfectly fine. Go to the quiet. You can mourn there and touch All that Is. In this place is the splendor of Being. Your heart is leading you. Listen. Know the motions you go through are not in vain.

You think of a baby now, Mary. But what does this really mean to you? Sadness? Are you over the pain of Grace's death? By moving on, you move on. Are you sad thinking that you will leave Grace behind? You sense that you must look to the future, turn your face to the sun, that change is on the horizon for you. It Is! Dear, dear Mary.

Hold on, for we are so very near. This writing is monumental for you and it takes courage. Hope. There is nothing wrong with hope. You despair—replace this with hope. Be true to the place that you are in. Embrace the very fact that you are human. Turn softly, move gently. Love is all around. You hear music—move into the music. You feel the sun on your cheek—move gently into the sun. You smile—feel the smile stay on your lips. You pray—feel the words of the prayer.

Know love by knowing yourself. Softness enters your being in realization, just as a doe moves into the mist on a summer's morning. Let the light shine on you. This new side has been hidden. Give it light. Savor this new friendship with an old friend. Your sadness has been keenly linked to your gentleness. Gentleness will remain for self when sadness leaves. The softness that you have sought for self is finally here, Mary dearest. Say Hello! You are finally reunited!

Thank you, Dear Ones.

Dearest Gracie,   January 26, 1996

Two weeks ago, Daddy and I were in Florida, on vacation again. It was a beautiful sunny day. I was on the beach; your grandparents and father were looking for seashells further up the shore. I watched the ocean. It was at that moment that I knew. I knew I might always cry for the child I lost. But I, as your mother, knew the spirit you have become.

I knew in those moments that I had given you all the

love I could possibly give. That I had been the best mother I knew how to be. I accepted that. My doubt had been just that. *My* doubt. Not God's. Not the doctors'. Not my family's. Not your father's. Mine.

I knew also in those moments that I had chosen to love. That as I turned my face to the wind, I would always choose love, from that day on. And if I lost my way again, I would know that I was never alone.

Grace, I turned a corner that day. That moment. Forgiveness had slipped in quietly one night and said, "I will lie with you, I am in your heart." I forgave myself. It was then that I knew I loved myself honestly and with truth. It was only then that I knew that God had been in my heart, always. I just had not been able to see.

Gracie, you gave me that. This love. This ability to see. This ability to embrace, put my arms around my humanity with love. The ripples of love are just beginning, aren't they?

February 3, 1996

Dear Trinity, Gracie, and the Holy Spirit,

I have thought so much about my dreams lately. It seems incredible to me that this part of my life has opened up, as it has. Each morning at work, Julie, Margaret, and I have what we call a "dream update." Each of us has been blessed somehow with this ability to dream.

I think of myself and how much is revealed to me in my dreams, how you are guiding me to these dreams and

159

through these dreams. It is as if I have been given clues that help to unlock the mysteries of my life. I want to thank you for this.

In my dream last night, John went to watch television in another room. Without my knowing how it happened, there was a piano in front of me. I started playing (even though I do not play in real life). I remember touching the keys and having beautiful music come out. It was as if I felt the notes. Each touch was wonderful—the tones were fantastic. I remember thinking, *But I can't even play the piano!* I then saw Margaret's piano right beside mine, also appearing miraculously. Her piano was different from mine, but equally beautiful. I then felt waves of ecstasy go through my body. Wave upon wave. I remember thinking, *No wonder Margaret likes to play the piano so much!* She, in reality, does not play piano, either.

Does this have anything to do with writing?

Always in love, ∾ Mary

Trinity,   February, 1995

Can we talk? Can we speak of my feelings? I need guidance with these feelings of sharing Grace with the world in the book that Margaret is writing about our friendships. . . . Please?

You are robbed of nothing. Let your emotions reign. Know that these feelings guide you. Your love is within—believe and treasure this. Allow this to unfold. Your search is over now. I mean over! There is nothing left to do. Allow yourself to feel the luxury of your gentleness, without pain or sadness. Your emotions are the way. Not blocking them releases them for you. It has been the stuffing of them through your past that has built up momentum and lowered your energy. All the emotions that have controlled you in the past will cease to be a burden.

The world of emotion now, as you pass through the gates of acceptance, allows you to see! Your sadness was only saying, FEEL YOUR GENTLENESS—FOR SELF. This is one of the reasons you have chosen sadness frequently—to allow yourself this gentleness. It was at these times you allowed yourself your humanness. Dishes piled up during these times. You took time off work to be. I am not speaking of the times you may have escaped, I am speaking of the times you were sad and did not mask it. You were gentle.

Now in this time, you can proceed with gentleness as your friend— without the need to choose sadness or pain. As you allow this for self, you allow this with others. You have lived with a shell of protection for so long. A scared little girl was hiding. You have been hidden so long, mostly from yourself.

Caress who you are and all will fall into place—including the book. What a special book this will be. You have lost nothing, my sweetheart. You have only gained. The shell is gone. You have taken it off. You have found the key!

Thank you, my beings of light. I will be sweet and gentle—to me.

March 5, 1996

Dearest Trinity, Gracie and the Angels
and the Holy Spirit,

I want to start by thanking you for today—the laughter,

the happiness at work, all of it. Julie, Margaret, and I just keep enjoying things more and more. Even our jobs! The most mundane parts of our jobs have somehow become filled with pleasure, in that we are sharing so much more.

I have recently thought of how little I sometimes thank you for things—how I just take things for granted, like I am out of touch or something. I want to thank you now. As a matter of fact, I did not thank you for the great dinner we had tonight. I am always so grateful that we can put food on the table. Please do not think I am not grateful. I am. But I thought of this, this not thanking, and how long I had been doing it. I also do not thank people when they help me at times. I want to practice being more thankful.

This file of Amanda's was highlighted just now. Is there something †hat I should do for her? I just saw the cross. Is that a yes? Can you shed light on this?

Know that what you do is all right, Mary. Know this. What are you thinking?

That I should be with her tonight. That you want me or are guiding me to do this tonight. And I struggle with this, this taking care of myself and taking care of her. I struggle with my wanting to write and having a child that may need me.

All is well. Love is there. You might ask yourself what is inside. Why would one think this?

162

Because of shoulds. Because that is how I have been raised.

It is. And simply that is it. It just Is. You ponder these things, these situations. Let them be. There is nothing that you need to worry about. Think of self and where these feelings lie. What do you want?

I want to write and rest and just be. That is all. But I feel guilty leaving Amanda. What should I do?

Just be, Mary. Allow these feelings to surface. This is fine. You are fine. Amanda is fine! Why do you question this guilt? What makes you feel guilty?

I think of things that I should be doing and am not doing, and I feel guilty. Whenever I want to be who I am, I feel guilty. Mostly, now, with people.

If you do what makes you happy, there is no room for guilt.

Now my neck is all wacky. I wonder if I am communicating †he right way. Oops, there is the cross again. You are with me, I know. Please guide me so that the decisions I make are for the highest good. You know, the more that I write, the more I am getting into this. It is almost interactive, isn't it?

I want to really let you know that my dreams are so fulfilling to me. Thank you! Especially the one with the interview. I really got a lot out of that one. In this dream, I see this man I know. He is well groomed, impeccably so. The perfect businessman. Not a hair out of place. A tough cookie. I was interviewing for a job with him. I saw this man as so gentle, not tough, as he appeared on the surface. I told him, "You have a big heart, you know." He hung his head, almost crumpling in his chair, and said, "I know." I asked him, "When did this happen?" He told me that this had happened with his last marriages. I then told him, "I have to be able to trust that this is a two-way street." He said he knew. There was such relief for him when he said this, when he heard the word *trust*. I was so happy that I did not want to wake up!

My sense is that I somehow play different roles in my dreams. I am all the characters of my dreams. This man was a side of me. The exact, precise, getting-the-job-done side. The perfectionist. The action side of my being that was so prevalent in my past. I saw this man saying his heart had been hurt by his past marriages, just as this part of me, my past marriage, or my other unions had been hurtful to me. I saw this man needing to have everything done perfectly. Always having to work, just like me. It was the productive side of who I had been for years.

You know, I just felt my anxiety lifting. I see now that I was carrying some guilt around—maybe because I felt I should have seen my grandmother tonight but didn't. I will do that tomorrow. But tonight I will do what pleases me. That makes me happy. I feel as if I can give more. Thank you for this insight.

I look at the angel wing card that I got from Nancy, my mother-in-law, and I think, *Wow, angel wings!* She sent me this just about the time I started feeling self-love. Thank you again. I finally understood that message today! It takes me some time. I love you all. Till next time.

March 1996

Dearest Angels, my Angel Grace, the Holy Spirit,

One of the reasons I have begun to include the Holy Spirit in these letters is because of another dream. In this dream, I am talking to someone. I hear a voice in response, but I do not see this person. Yet I know we are having a conversation. I know that this conversation has been going on for some time. It dawns on me during this talk that I am talking to the Holy Spirit! I say in the dream, "Oh, so *you* are the Holy Spirit." And that was the end of this dream.

This all seems so incredible to me. When I was talking to this voice, I felt as if I were talking to some friend or someone very familiar. I could not believe that I could be that relaxed with the *Holy Spirit*. And I am not even religious!

I really feel as if you have opened up my dream life— all of you. Thank you for all the help that you have given me.

March 6, 1996

Dearest Angels, my Gracie, Trinity, and the Holy Spirit,

I want to thank you again for my day and for the wonderful way Amanda and I are able to talk. It means so much to me and, I know, to her. This is what being a mother is all about to me. The best part is that I can use some of the lessons I have learned through all of you and through my dreams. These lessons are giving my life meaning now. Thank you.

At work, everything is more than I could have hoped for. Things are just flowing, and I feel freer. I see my goodness now. I see it in the eyes of others, and I want to give more and more. It helps so much to give to myself. I think of how many times I never gave to me. I always made sure someone else was taken care of first when what I have really craved was giving to myself. I never realized that I had to give to myself in order to truly give to others. That would have appeared too selfish in my eyes. I just kept trying to be better and better—until I was just a shell of who I was. No wonder I would wake up angry so frequently. No wonder I struggled internally. There was a side of me that needed attention so desperately. Thank you. Is there anything else that I should be aware of?

Listen, Mary. Listen to your heart and follow your heart. Do you hear? These are the things that we speak of.

I guess that I cannot hear.

You can hear. Listen. Pay attention to what you hear.

"To be born again." These are the words of a Van Morrison song. I can only hear the words and not what is inside of me. Is this what you mean?

We speak of distractions at this moment. Do you have distractions in your life? Listen to your heart. What does it say?

I guess that I am not quite hearing.

Relax. This will come. You have great wisdom inside. You know so much that you can share with the world. You are at the point at which you can share this with the world. Do you not feel this?

Yes, I feel something. Some deep connection. Something that is so right. What does this mean?

Listen, you will be guided. You can do this, Mary. Listen to your heart. We are here with you at this moment. You can count on us being with you at this time. Do not think for a moment that you will be left alone. We will guide you.

Okay. I will listen to my heart. I hope that I heard everything right here. Please stay with me. I need you all so much at this time. I must go. I'll see you in my dreams.

March 9, 1996

Dearest Angels, Gracie, Trinity, the Holy Spirit,

Please watch over me, if you feel that it is for the highest good. I would like this writing to be what it should be—what it is. Something for the world. Please guide my fingers and thoughts. I really need you. You guide me so much throughout the day.

You know that the more I write, the more I love writing and that, in and of itself, is so wonderful. Thank you for John and my friends and Amanda. I want to write my feelings for her soon, so she can see how much I love her. I learn so much from her.

Mary, you are guided. Say no more. We are here with you and always will be. Forever and ever. Let yourself feel the words, let yourself be. There is nowhere that you have to get to. And the story is still unfolding, as it always will be. These thoughts that you reflect on are there for a reason. Follow that reason and you will be there. This is the natural part of your writing—the heart. You have recognized that you are so much from the heart. This was hidden from you in the past. It has now revealed itself for you because you have chosen love. Yes! Your writing is different because you are different in love. But all of this is necessary for the story to unfold. The rest of the story contains the light that others seek. Allow this to show through. You are in a different place and time now. This is fine! It is to be celebrated. Rejoice in love!

Thank you dearest Angels, my Trinity, and Gracie, and the Holy Spirit. I love you all. Here I go with the writing. Wish me luck!

March 12, 1996

Dearest Trinity, Gracie, my dear Angels,
and the Holy Spirit,

I want to thank you. I had my friends over today. It has been so long since this has happened—since Grace's death. Margaret sent off her book, about our friendships (Julie's, hers, and mine) and the connections we have shared, to the publisher today. She is very excited about this and wants so much for it to be published. I wish this for her also. Thank you for all the help.

I am sitting here wondering what is going to be happening with me and this purpose stuff. Did my dream of the porpoises have anything to do with any of this? Swimming with my "purposes," side by side?

Mary, all dreams have to do with the reflection of purpose. The mirror. The being. YOU ARE SO RIGH† WHEN YOU EXAMINE THESE MEANINGS.

I just lost my thoughts. I saw the cross again. Is this my purpose? The cross? God? I mean in the literal sense? I have been seeing crosses everywhere. It may mean God is in my life, sacredness, all of you. . . . Am I on the right track?

You are on the right track. God is in your life. In your heart. This is so. Relax, Mary. You are thinking too hard. This is not something difficult, dear one. You are right when you know that it is something close to you, in front of you.

Are you saying "in front of me" meaning the computer? Is it something with the computer? Is it writing? Is it my thoughts?

You have so much to share at this point. Think of how you can share. This is what you will endeavor to do. Share. Now, sharing comes in many different forms.

Will I be sharing my ideas?

You already are. You are sharing with Julie and Margaret now. This will increase. This sharing will increase. This sharing is so much a part of you. You will see. Doors will open for you in this realm. You will share. You will share so much.

Will I speak?

Yes. You will speak.

Is this about what we have seen? been through?

You will see!

Should I prepare in any way for this to occur?

You need not do anything. Just be open. Things are coming to you rapidly. You sense this.

I cannot figure this out. I have to let this go. I have a sense of drifting, of things almost being on hold, as if this is all right. I am getting tired now. I feel as if I really need to go to sleep and yet it is so early.

Thank you so much. Thank you! And thank you for helping me get out into the world. I think I am ready. I love you all so much. You make my life so worth living. Thank you. I love you all.

March 14, 1996

Dearest Angels, Trinity, Gracie, and the Holy Spirit,

I give thanks because of what is happening to my friends at work. Margaret is so happy with the book she has completed and I am happy for her. She is so ready to be an author, if this is for the highest good. And Julie is getting new energy and feeling so content. It really is good to see them like this.

Yet, I see this, and I wish it for myself at times. Not to take anything away from their happiness. I wish that I could know what my purpose is. I am getting into doubt at times. Do I have a talent? I mean something that I can do? I feel as if I could cry now. Why is this? Can you help me? Am I selfish? I feel as if I do not have anything to offer. I am stumped.

Mary, be. You are not alone and never will be. Allow things to come forth and they will. Time is here as a teacher for you. You are not selfish. You only feel this. You are. You want what all want. To understand what life holds and is about. Think of how far you have come in such a short time. Is this not a miracle?

Miracles come in all shapes and sizes. You experience these daily. Yet you want verification. It Is. So let these feelings arise within you. Give them air. You are ready to breathe. Ready to be ready. This is fine. You search and search and think and think. Where does this take you? To more searching and thinking. This is fine, but it can wear one out. Be and It will be. Dearest, all the answers are within you. Everything you search for is already there! Clear your vision.

I am unhappy because I do not have Grace and it appears to me that everyone I know has children and I don't. I guess I have been angry. I know that I can't make things happen that are not in the divine plan. Yet I feel so sad. I also know that a child is not the one and only answer for me. Is there something I am missing? Please help me. My throat just aches now. Have I been so awful that this is happening to me?

Your sadness has been with you since Margaret told you of her daughter's car accident and how she got the phone call that nothing had come of this accident. You wanted this to be how your life went. That with one phone call, you were told that all was well, even though something had occurred. This is fine, dearest Mary. To have these feelings indicates you're being human. This is your beauty—your humanness. People relate to you on such a human level. Yes, you can hide your emotions, but when you choose to reveal them, they ring with such humanness.

It is amazing that when one gives something voice, it can then leave. You have given your sadness voice. It can leave and it will. This I can guarantee you. Never forget that one of your greatest gifts is the ability to connect to people. This is your beauty! Your love! Mary, when you are who you are, you will not want. You have traveled this road. You know what it involves. Be who you are. Know this is the most comforting of decisions for you.

When something comes to mind, ask, "How can I be me? Who am I now?" And it will be. You will be. It is as if you have a list of what you should be, and if a part of you is not on the list, you panic. You punish yourself. Relax. Sadness and happiness and joy and wonder are all on the list. There is only one list.

Truth lies in who you are. Let this be known.

Thank you for all of this. I will practice being who I am at all times. And I will attempt being true. Thank you for this insight. I love you.

March 20, 1996

Dearest Angels, Trinity, Gracie, and the Holy Spirit,

I must tell you why I have come today. I have had a major breakthrough of sorts. I need your assistance, Trinity. I would like to discuss my dream of last night.

In this dream, I am in an elevator going up. In the elevator are my mother and Margaret's mother, Madeline. We are on the way to a college party. I remember feeling very emotionally wounded and hurt. I felt so empty, as if I were some type of pinball being bumped around. The man I was seeing wanted only a physical relationship from me. He didn't want *me*—who I really was. This hurt me deeply. This felt like such a random period in my life.

I press the button and then all of a sudden the elevator goes sideways. I grab on to Madeline's wrist. She looks upset with me when I do this.

The wrist is a connecting point. A point that connects the hand with the body. To hold on to the connecting point is significant, Mary. To hold on to Madeline's wrist is significant. Comfort is significant. To hold on to the wrist of a mother is significant. Madeline is also your mother's friend. To hold on to a friend is highly significant. The fact that she is female is significant. Examine this now.

Could it be that I was holding on to a friend, the female part of me? And then Madeline got a little miffed for my doing that—that in itself seems significant. The female mother, friend, old friend that is not used to me wanting comfort from her. My female side needing comfort. The

173

fact that it was not my mother that I held on to was important, I feel. Is this so?

YES! YES! YES! You chose to hold on to an old friend in need. An older woman, mother, friend—all are significant. You are reclaiming the part of you that was ignored—the female side. The side that needs to give you much. From this point, you will see how to view and treat yourself by just being. By just receiving. You need not worry about action, as in the male side. You have not been in the female side. You have rejected that in the past to survive. This was necessary at one time but is no longer. This is hugely significant! You need to be able to receive! By that act of reaching, and reaching only, you are reclaiming. You reached out for someone else to receive comfort.

And the party with people from my past?

You were revisiting your past and a painful part of your life. This may have been one of the most painful times you experienced, the most lost you have ever felt. This was necessary to revisit. And in the revisiting you reached out for comfort from Madeline. You hung on to someone, an older, wiser woman, a female. These are symbols for you.

You are reviewing your past and going back to these moments to give them new meaning. Congratulations! You have rewritten a part of your life! This will help you in your view of self. Your interpretations are excellent. This will benefit you greatly in the future! Now write and we will be with you.

Thank you, my dear angels.

Trinity, March 1996

I had another dream, I need help—once again. In this

dream, I see a rat in the garage of the home from my first marriage. The rat was called Bluebeard. This old rat had long whiskers and blue-gray fur. He even looked almost friendly. The whole dream seemed so odd.

I knew nothing of this Bluebeard, until I asked John about it last night. It appears this is a legend about a man who was rumored to have killed his ex-wives. Bluebeard then married a young woman and forbade her to go into many rooms in the castle where he kept his former wives as part of his past. The hidden part of his life. Well, as the legend goes, the new wife went into the forbidden rooms one by one, bringing each wife out to the light. Yet, in knowing her husband's secret, she still loved him. And consequently, she lived. But she too became part of the past. . . .

Could this have anything to do with my female side being "put down" or suppressed symbolically? Somewhere in my past life—my past marriage? I feel this, too, was done for protection. I grieve the fact that I have done this to myself. I feel now that I want balance. That this is what has been out of whack for me. The yin-yang of it all. Am I on to something?

Mary, this is why you grieve. Your heart cries out for this balance. You know this balance, and these dreams are lessons for you to rewrite what has occurred. It is time to give up what you knew, what you thought was real, to proceed into the future with integration. With oneness. Have you not had recent dreams in which you reached out to the female for help? You know this is important, that this is so! This is all to assist you in this transformation. This change of being. You know! Therefore, you are. Do not be afraid to ask for this to be so.

Will you assist me in this transformation of self? with this integration of being? with this knowing? this move toward oneness? I feel that the barriers I once had are coming down. This makes me so happy, and I am able to trust myself so much more with this! Thank you!

Of course, Mary, we will help! We know that you are at this point. Believe me when I say your life will become infinitely better, easier, loving, embracing, wondrous! Dearest, cherish this point in time. Know how significant this is! Ask and it shall be. Do you not already feel some of the tension is gone? What you held on to is gone? It can happen that quickly! Move into this realm. We are there for you. We love you so!

Thank you, dearest Ones. My heart is with you. I am with you. Love surrounds us all in oneness. Thank you for all this wisdom. I will ponder. I love you all.

Dearest Grace and Trinity,   March 22, 1996

Every time that I see the number twenty-two, I think of you, Grace. It is the number of your birthdate, and today is March 22. Last night, in my dream, I got a new white bathing suit. It was beautiful and I felt great in it. I put it on and then John appeared. Each time I took a step, your father would give me a kiss. With each step I took. He kept kissing me all the way.

When I awoke it struck me that John represents the male side of my nature—once again. With this dream, it appears that the male side of me is loving the other side of me (the female) and with each new step I take, I feel this love.

I ask myself, have I really ever been able to receive? Receptivity is so symbolically female. I have always been the "doer." But if dreams are any reflection of my internal life, it looks to me as if I have begun to allow this receptivity.

The aspect of my being in a white bathing suit, white denoting purity, and that it was a "bathing" suit could mean that I am cleansing the doing side of myself—the male. The action side. Those kisses from John show me that my male side is at last working in tandem with the female side. Somehow I am beginning to balance myself.

I cannot tell you how this makes me feel.

Thank you, Angels!

Dear Trinity and Grace,   March 24, 1996

I come, once again, with news of dreams. My world has opened up, so completely. I have to share this with you.

I dreamed I saw a woman walking toward me. She came from quite a distance, as if she were only a speck on the horizon. Everything was bright about her, even her clothing. She appeared beautiful, but I could not see her clearly. We kept approaching one another until I recognized her. This woman was me.

I began to cry when I realized I saw myself in a "perfect light." I knew that she had come to tell me we were the best of friends. We spoke through our minds. As I approached her we blended into one another—our bodies just became one.

I have never felt such complete happiness. Never, ever, ever. . . .

How can this get any better?

IV.
FINDING

MIRACLES

April 2, 1996

Dearest Angels, Gracie my love, Trinity,
and the Holy Spirit,

I had a wonderful day yesterday. I know that so much
is about to take place. I feel excited somehow. I pray that
Margaret's book will get published, as I am sure it will.
Thank you for my dear Amanda. I love her with all my
heart. Please watch over her and bring her love, Gracie.
She needs to realize how special she truly is. I will help
where I can.

I also ask that you watch over John. He needs to know

that he can also be creative, should he choose to be. We both can. It is the biggest gift to realize this. I would wish that we could have a family that loved what they do— who are doing what they truly want. I have this wonderful jazz on now. I feel just wonderful! Guess what? No tears! Just smiles!

I ask that you guide my sister, Liz, as she has her new baby. I will be at the hospital with her. I wish her the best. Now I am crying. Oh well, so much for the smiles! I guess you can have both—happiness and tears. Is there anything that I should be aware of?

We speak of writing here, Mary. Let us examine this writing. What is it you want the world to know about your love for your daughter?

That all continues. That love transcends time and space. That I have learned so much on this journey with Grace. That I am a better person to myself because of my love for her. That having you and Grace and the Holy Spirit in my life has made it worth living. That we maybe cannot understand all, but that there is a reason for everything. We just may not see it at the time. That love is all there is! I feel it! I am living proof of it!

You are right, Mary, when you say that love resides within you. This is important. Keep this in mind always. Love is within you. Always. Love is transforming. You know that is what we speak of here. All the judgments of the past have gone. You speak of how hard you are on your selves on this physical plane. This is what we speak of here. The freedom to choose not pain but joy! To choose joy! This can be done. Others need to understand that this can be done! You can show them and help them with this lesson, this journey. The journey of choice! Do not forget that you can continue to write. You can still guide people with this knowledge. The knowledge of choice. We will be here for you, dearest. We love you so.

And I all of you! Kisses to you and my angel daughter! I just saw a highlighted file with Messages in it, with a story that I had written or started. Is there something that I should know?

We speak of your story now. It is true that you have gotten the message—the message of love, dearest. Do not fear. This is to let you know that we are here beside you, within you, to help you should you need help with the rest of the story. This is a big step for you—the act of revealing. This act alone will set so much in motion.

You feel now the comfort of love. You see this revealed in your family. You see how you look at John differently because you look at yourself differently. You notice Amanda in a different light because you see yourself in a different light. So much has changed for you through this love. This is the transformation we speak of.

Thank you, my angels. I depend on you for all of this. Please help me when I write. I really need you to be close to me, guiding me all the way. If I get a little nervous, know that I need you to help me. I know that I can count on you. I know that you are with me always. You are in my heart.

This is an open invitation to let you know that we are here for you! Do not forget that. Realize, Mary. Realize, dear one. The spirit is free.

Thank you for the invitation. I will need you this weekend, if not sooner. Can you help me with this writing? We can work together. I love you my dears!

April 5, 1996

Dearest Angels, my Daughter, Trinity,
and the Holy Spirit,

I want to thank you for tonight. It is Good Friday and I went to church with Margaret. Although I was not raised Catholic, I found the music, which I think was sung in the ancient language Aramaic, to be beautiful. I found myself crying—not needing to understand the words but only to hear the sounds. They were beautiful. I found that church to be so human in that people worship so openly. It just seems as if nothing is hidden. The reenactment of taking Jesus off the cross was so moving.

When we left the church, I looked up to a beautiful dark blue sky with stars. You could tell that spring would come soon. The air held a warmth to it for me. I thought, when I was at church, of Grace's name and how in Spanish it would be *gracias,* meaning "thanks." I thought of how I had been born on Thanksgiving Day, and how thankful I was that Grace was in my life. That is all that matters. Grace is in my life. . . .

Later that night . . .

Dearest Trinity,

I am back again. I could not stay away—for some reason I could not sleep. I want to thank you for the good news Margaret had from a publisher about her book. It is wonderful and we all felt the joy last night. Deb, Margaret, and I celebrated and toasted and laughed. Well, I am sure you were there! I have been happy today, and then I get a little wistful. And then I think of the book and I get excited. I had told Margaret she could name the book *Grace* if she wanted to. Now I feel wistful about this.

Mary do not fear. Follow your heart. Your heart will lead you. You have these thoughts because you miss your dear daughter and feel, Well, this is all I have of Grace—her name. *But she is so much more than a name, dearest. It is this that we speak of. She is Grace! The Grace of God! Could she not have a more perfect name? John named her. This name came to him for a reason. Your story will be told, dearest. It is with this love that you will see. You have been so selfless to share so much of this with others. This pain. This tragedy. This love! It takes much to be able to do this. Grace feels all of this and knows what you go through. How you have struggled to share your only child. The child you cannot hold. Grace knows all of this, Mary.*

Trinity's voice becomes silent. My fingers hover over the computer keys waiting. I listen. The pause continues. I then hear a completely new voice that says,

"Mama, I love you so. . . ."

And I begin to cry.

GRACE

Icontinue to listen to the words of this voice. Tears begin streaming down my cheeks. My hands begin trembling. I try again to understand. I have never heard any other voice but that of Trinity. Yet I cannot stop writing.

My mind wants to tell my fingers to stop, but I can't. I keep recording what is being said. . . .

I am with you. We are bound together through the cord of love. This will be for always and eternity. Do not fear, for I am with you. I stand by you now. The light that you have seen has been me. I, too, could not be parted from you. We are together now. And always will be. Oh,

GRACE

Mother of mine, how I know you long to hear me call your name. I have. I have. I have called your name!

Thank you for the time we had together on this earth. I saw all the love you were and are! I saw how much you cared. I saw you grieve. I saw it all, Mama! Do you not see how we are not parted? How our love has kept us together? That the strength of your love came through? That is how powerful this love is, my mother. You know only love with me and I with you.

I begin to answer. . . .

Gracie, when I look at your photograph, I cry because I remember all those tubes. It was so hard for me, so difficult for you. To see you like that. [My tears are dripping down to the computer keys, on my hands. I try to blow my nose. I keep writing, and I don't know why.]

I know we are together Grace. The power of my love for you . . . I would have done anything to find you, to know that you were safe. I would have climbed the highest mountain for you. [I keep attempting to grasp what I have heard. I continue writing.]

Gracie, this is all about love and you have taught me that, darling. I love you so very much and I am so proud of you. Look at how you have affected so many people and how many more will be affected. This is what your love has done for people. Given love. Stay with me, my little girl. Because I will never leave you. It's just you and me. Me and my baby. Please stay with me. . . .

I then kiss the screen of the computer.

Dearest Trinity and Grace, April 6, 1996

I do not understand. I don't know why this is happening to me—this experience of last night left me with the exact same sensations as that time when the computer scrolled. I feel as if my mind is reeling. How can this be?

Please, Trinity and Grace. Help me. I am in no-man's land here. I need guidance fast. Please help me.

April 7, 1996

Dearest Angels, Gracie, Trinity, and the Holy Spirit,

Thank you for this Easter. It has been wonderful to be with my family and with John. This is all that matters to me. I loved the conversation around the dinner table today when I could talk about this stuff, the stuff of angels and life and love and what it means to be human. I am so proud of Margaret and the book. She does have a true gift in that she can write such beautiful words and collect all the concepts with such detail. I am not cut from that cloth. But I can talk! I can spread the word of love to all! Just give me a chance and I will! John calls me "bunny" now. The rabbit in Native American symbolism means conquering fear. Boy does that sound good. And you know what? I am! I am conquering fear!

Gracie, I still wonder about what went on the other night. I can't help but wonder. Was that really you?

I will write later.

Dearest Gracie,   April 8, 1996

I am going to attempt to speak with you again. I have so many questions.

Gracie, you know that I miss you. You know that I am trying to understand this. Sometimes it is so difficult when I miss you. If you can hear me, please could you explain any of this? What is going on with me?

Mother, dearest one. Do not despair over your emotions. This is the way in which you recognize your humanness. This is a very big step for you to come to me and cross the barrier of infant to spirit. Yet your love brings you here tonight. It is with love that we can speak to one another. You have so much to give the world. There is no need to blame yourself for anything. Ever. There is no need to blame. Your spirit is free. You know this now. This is a time for celebration! My dear Mother, how I love you! Realize that without belief we could not be corresponding. You would not be able to hear me. But you do hear me. This is what Trinity meant when he said to listen. And you did! You can hear! We will continue these conversations. This I know. All it takes is love, my dearest.

You say to self, "But how can this be? How can I speak to my daughter who is in the arms of God?" But it is so. This is as real as what you can see. You can hear. This is real, my Mother. For so long you did not trust what you saw with the computer. This is real, my Mother. With love so much can be seen! We are together. Let your spirit go with this realization. Do you not feel lighter now? Do you not feel that we are together? For we are together. Do not fret that this is unusual to understand. Love has brought you to this place. And with love we will continue to grow.

GRACE

There is no limit to the love we feel for one another. Do not put limits on your love. Your gift to the world is your love. Your love is so vast, like the oceans. Rejoice, Mother. When I say rejoice, you know that I speak the truth. I am surrounded by nothing but love. And when I see your love, I sing! Just as when you see the love of Amanda or my father, you sing! You really do! If sadness touches you, know that love is there also. It is there. You can choose to love, my Mother. You can choose.

But Gracie, what about the aspect of duality? Why do we have that? I know it is to learn from, but . . .

The duality, or opposites, can be but an illusion when one sees that all there is is love. You know this to be true with the oneness. When you have transcended a certain issue in life, there is integration. What was fragmented becomes whole. One. You move above the two. It ceases to matter. Day/night, darkness/light, good/evil, all revolves around love.

Grace, this is hard to understand. I have read that we have duality on earth because we have time. Are you saying that we can get to a place where there is no time, no opposites?

Time and duality are both illusions. In time, there appears to be past and future. In reality, this is experienced simultaneously, as one entity, the Eternal Now. This state may be reached by stepping "out of time," by going to the stillness of being—by cascading inward, for all your riches are truly inside, not out. Duality, or opposites, is illusionary. For life in reality cannot be "in opposition" to itself. This would totally negate life. In spirit, there are no opposites. Everything that appears in opposition has become one. The illusion is that there was ever two to begin with. When you see love in hatred, you have risen above the opposites. When you see the light within the dark, you have risen above opposites.

Mother, this is in the stillness. It is in being. It is in the sacred space of knowing. There is transcendence. There can be heaven on earth. This is what humankind strives for. It is peace on earth. You have felt peace in your heart. There is nothing sweeter in life—to know all is at peace within.

Gracie, I feel calmer by talking to you. Can we do this again? I thought that I was losing my faith, when really I was trying to understand this phenomenon, this ability to speak with my infant daughter. This has really helped me, darling. Has it helped you?

Oh, Mother, all your love aids me, feeds me, nourishes my spirit! This is what I have waited for! To be close to you! To have you know that I am here for you!

Things have been so intense for me at work and person-ally, lately. I may just have to rest for a while. I have to also take care of myself. And Liz is having her baby. Can you be there if you are not too busy? It would mean a lot to me. You, too, dearest Trinity! Gracie, this has eased my loneliness for you a few minutes ago. Thank you, dear daughter.

Your mother and friend, kisses to you, darling. Just like I used to do at the hospital.

April 11, 1996

Dearest Angels, Gracie, Trinity, and the Holy Spirit,

I want to thank you for bringing Margaret and Julie to me. Without them, without their love and support, I could not have made it as far as I have. Thank you.

Today Margaret told me to be human. I realized that the only time I had no shame with my sadness and anger was when Grace was alive. I had no shame. When I said those words, I realized that I had so much shame about being human now, even in my own eyes. When Liz had her baby, I felt so much sadness, and I was trying so hard to be happy. Oh, I get all mixed up sometimes.

I guess I still feel a little sad. I think part of this is anger. I just asked my anger what I could learn from it, and I heard "compassion." That made so much sense to me. Compassion. Will you help me with my compassion for self? I really need some help, if you feel this is for the higher good.

Mama, I hear you. I am here near you now. Let us talk. Do not despair. There is so much that you have been through and are trying to integrate. Do not despair!

First, let us speak of motherhood. This issue has weighed heavily on your mind. First and foremost, you are a mother, a mother now. Think of what you have with this motherhood. I speak of Amanda now and how you have opened her up. So much of her trust of self stems from the fact that you have helped her to see the light. Continue to do this. This is your gift to her. This helps her to love herself. This helps you to love yourself. You both need this love. Now!

GRACE

Mother, love the fact that you love. And you love so sweetly. You bring so much joy to others. Why do think you have gotten so much love back in this time of need? Because of all the love that you have given so selflessly for years. This is all being reflected back to you. Now!

My Mother, you are breaking free of the chains that have held you. Celebrate, my dearest! You are free. Today when you spoke with Margaret and Julie, you had an epiphany. You realized where your pain and sadness stemmed from and, hence, your anger. Without this capability, you were unable to move on.

Now let us speak of what it means to be a mother in the future. Where will this take you? Are you ready for this, Mama? Where would you like to go with this? Envision yourself there. Envision yourself with a baby, a beautiful baby. Let this vision take you into the future. Let this love await you there! Yes, you are so right to see a woman pushing her child in the sun. In white! With love! Laughing, yes! All you want, my dearest! This is you! This is you!

Mama, your fear has kept you in a place of not being able to choose. But there is always choice. Know that you can always choose! I chose you and you chose me. We wanted to be together and it is still this way. Nothing can part us. Not now, dearest. Not with faith.

Mother, you know that your thoughts have been my thoughts for so long. That you have recognized my voice from a place of love. That you have heard me in your thoughts. That in so many ways I am your thoughts. You know that none of this was punishment meant for you. This was a road of choice decided long ago. With love. You said, "I will remember," and you have! You have remembered to love, always love.

You know that on the day of my death, your dream was sent to you. To give you hope. Pure hope, my mother. And it did. You could not forget the dream. The feeling of the dream. The divinity! This is what we speak of. Although my father held me in his arms with so much love, you felt what I felt. In death. You have felt that love, Mama.

So do not despair! You know the love of the divine! I want you to know that with this love, you will always choose love. For there is no other way. That is the way. When in doubt, ask one simple question: "How can I love myself?" And your road will be clear, your vision will be filled with joy, your ears will hear the songs of angels. For, dearest mother, you are such an angel. I mean this from my heart! Such an angel. As you unwrap the things that have bound you and cast them aside, you will notice that your movements become filled with ease. Already you have picked up the flow and how that has been part of your life. You will see this everywhere. With love, dearest.

Enjoy your life! Take time to play, and I mean play! Do what makes you happy! Live and love! Do you not see how this has affected your love with my father? With Amanda? Can you not see how this has touched so many parts of your life? And it always has. All aspects of life contain lessons. Now is your time to enjoy the lessons of love. So love! And I will love right beside you!

Thank you, darling! Gracie, I feel that if you were a grown woman or my friend we would naturally be so close. Is this so?

Mother, there is a reason that we were mother and daughter. There is a huge reason. The first being choice—the choice of love. Our love runs so deep, Mother, it has come through the physical world to the divine to express itself. The second reason is that our lessons were so needed, and we chose to learn them together. There is often more than the obvious in terms of how one learns, how one reflects one's purpose. You say, "But my daughter died." How do you know that you have not chosen to help others on their path? From one incident that you judged yourself so strongly about, how do you know that you might not have had a divine purpose? Things unfold in their own time. You have always sensed something so right about yourself. And this is what kept your belief, your faith alive. When others may have doubted, you did not. There may have been moments when you faltered, but you got right back on the path.

Gracie, I know I chose you. When you were just a little dream in my mind, I knew I would have an angel—I love you darling.

April 12, 1996

Dearest Angels, my Gracie, Trinity, and the Holy Spirit,

I want to thank all of you for helping me and for helping Margaret and Julie. There was so much love and happiness in the workplace today! Julie had a dream in which a barrier was being taken away, with Margaret at the wheel of a rental truck. And I have been able to feel compassion for myself. I have been able to speak to my dear daughter Grace. This makes me so happy. Gracie, I am so in awe and so happy for this. That we can communicate! It means so much to me. And the song that Julie heard, "Hail Mary, Full of Grace," that is how I felt—full of Grace.

Gracie, you know that as I drove home I had thoughts that this is enough—to know that we can communicate. That if there are no other children for Dad and me, I have had you. And that makes me so happy. You were everything to me and still are. To think that we can still communicate brings me such profound relief. That I do not have you in physical form does not mean the love stops there. It feels alive.

And so are we, even if, maybe, in different dimensions. Can I thank you enough? Can I thank Trinity enough for helping with this process? Can I thank the other Angels who are so important in helping me to balance and helping me to forgive and reclaim lost parts of myself? Can I thank the Holy Spirit for bridging the way for all this divinity to become manifested in my life? My heart thanks you.

Dearest Mother, we stand beside you now. Our hearts blend with yours in this moment, this moment of realization and love. It is truly an honor to be a part of this, we all feel this! Your journey has been one of strife, at times, yet you survive to tell this story—this story of love and growth. We view this and feel the pride of knowing you know, the love of knowing you know and can assist others on their way if you so choose. This is such a monumental time for all. For Julie, who has connected through love, her barriers are down. She need not worry any longer. For Margaret, whose strength and belief have surrounded both you and Julie. This time brings joy to all! And all of you feel this! Do you not think there is a reason that all of you have come to this point of joy?

Let us speak, my dear Mother, of suffering, which you have been considering of late. Why, you ask, is there suffering? What purpose, you ask, does it serve? Why must humankind go through this suffering? These are such enormous yet simple questions. You have lived this question, my mother. Do you not see?

Why did you go through suffering? To learn. Does one choose suffering? Yes, but not in the way you may imagine. Suffering is chosen when one feels one has no choice. That this is how it is. Everyone chooses.

But Grace, why? How—with your life and death, with natural disasters, things of this nature, how can people choose this?

People choose which lessons they want to learn for their evolution. Is it love they want to learn? Compassion? They choose. One is constantly evolving on all planes. You are so right when you say that we all keep evolving even after death, one can go higher and higher, always.

But Grace, if, as you said last night, things are not always obvious in terms of the big plan, that someone may offer themselves, their life, for something they are unaware of at the time, then how can they choose suffering? I mean, even though they may have had to suffer. As I think of myself, I ask, did I choose this? Because I had no choice? Or thought I had no choice? What?

It is both, Mother. You felt you had no choice and you also wanted to serve. You felt you had no choice on the physical plane. But on the spiritual plane, you wanted to serve. You have always wanted to serve others, and you have—so nobly. You came to the physical plane to learn. You have learned and will continue to do so. On the spiritual plane, you have known what your destiny has always been and is: to serve with love. To be with love. You are integrating both worlds: the physical and the divine.

You know, Grace, that I have trusted you and my love for

you as no other. I know you know that, but I had to tell you. This trust is what really clued me in as to how deep our connection is, because I have never trusted as I do now, until I had you. It started with you. I have never had the ability to love, really love, until I had you. I came close with your father and my family but you know how relationships add that other dimension of learning together. And then you were born and died and I had to live on this trust.

But what really astounds me is that our love crosses all barriers of time and space. And that you heard me! Gracie, Mother loves you so! I do so much darling! I think of you as this wonderful spirit angel. And you have come to me with so much love. We must have really loved one another. And still do. But this seems like such a miracle to me!

It is a miracle, Mother. All miracles occur through love. Remember this! You know now that you can choose. And in so doing can have love in your life. All of you can have so much love in your lives.

I feel that there is much we can discuss here on these pages. That these pages are filled with love. That I can learn so much, that maybe this can help others. What do you think, Grace?

Mother, I think that we are always learning, growing—on these pages, off these pages, in our hearts, and with love. One grows through love. One transforms through love. One knows through love! This I know!

All I know, dear daughter, is that I am so happy to be able

to do this. I am so grateful to be able to do this. It is such a big relief for me to be able to do this. Thank you!

You know, today, when Julie told me she had heard that song, "Hail Mary," and I had signed my name to you last night as your mother, Mary, I knew that to be a sign that we truly were in communication. I saw this great connection. You know that sometimes I do not remember what I have written on these pages when I talk to angels. The impact is felt days later. So when I get those signs, it helps so much. Thank you for that. Please thank God for me for you. I know that God knows, but for the record—this has meant the world to me. Oh, dear Angels! Thank you for coming into my heart! Thank you, Holy Spirit!

Gracie,   April 22, 1996

I am having problems. I don't want my confusion to alarm you. You know that I have been trying to get all this straight in my mind, with my being able to talk to you. I hope that you understand all this. I love you so and I am trying to understand, and I do; I keep reading your words. I miss you, Grace, although I know that you are with me. Thank you for this.

Mother, this is an honor that we speak together. I understand your confusion. Know that I stand by you always, should you need me. I am here for you. I love you so very, very much, dearest. Nothing can take that away. We are here together for a very special reason. That reason is love. Can I tell you that the amount you miss me is the amount of love you will feel—even more. Your heart beats with a pureness and openness that makes me sing. I see you and I smile. I see how you make others laugh and how you bring your gentleness into their hearts. Dear Mother, how can any child want more from a mother? How can any child not say with pride, "This is my Mother!"?

Gracie darling, I am crying so hard I can hardly type. My head hurts now. When I was a little girl, my mother used to say that we could put a cold washcloth on our eyes so they would not look so red after we cried. If you were here with me in human form, we could do that. But I will not get into that. I wish you were in human form sometimes, but what can you do? I am just glad that we can speak.

Mama, listen to me. When you are outside with the flowers and the ground and are just thinking, I will be so very close to you. You will be able to feel me. Think of this the next time you are outdoors. Why do you think that Amanda brought up the name of Persephone when you were looking at the flowers last August? I will be so close. You think now of the robin in the tree last spring—this also was a sign for you. Only for you, my dear, dear Mother!

Gracie, what do you think of these letters? Are they okay for you? What do you think?

Mother, this is wonderful, incredible, so miraculous—you will see how miraculous this truly is! I will help you! We will do this together. Just me and you, me and my mama. Do not fear, for it is done. We will do this together.

Thank you, Grace. I still struggle when we speak. You know that this all seems so very huge to me. And yet I have to be close to you, in any way possible. If this is the way, then this is the way. Dear girl, dear angel, I love you so much, Gracie! I keep crying, even now. I know that someday we will be together and this will all seem like some dream, but until then, my angel, know that you are the best thing that ever happened to me. Gracie, you have opened my heart up so much.

Will you please, if you can, help your father? He seems so confused about what he wants with his music. If this is for the highest good. Let him know that I love him.

Mother, this is done. It would be an honor to help my father. Know that he will be fine. He struggles, as you have in the past. But he is on the road. He will find his way. Do not doubt that for an instant. I am part of this family too! We all work together to stay together. Do you feel better now, my dear one?

I do, Gracie! I feel happy that we have been able to do this, sweetheart. A kiss for you from me. Know that I adore you.

And I you Mother!

Good night, Gracie and my Angels and Trinity. I love you all! Thanks!

April 23, 1996

Dear Angels, Gracie, Trinity, the Holy Spirit,
and the Universe,

I just reread the above passage. I look at those words and they evoke so much feeling inside of me. Me talking to Grace. I am so grateful, please do not get me wrong. It is just that I have doubted some, these past days, because of this. Because I had a baby and now I can talk to the baby. What does it all mean? Here I am, talking to my daughter who died. She was so tiny, and now she is giving me advice and wisdom. Why do I doubt at times and yet cry when I read the words?

Same day . . .

Dearest Angels, Trinity, Gracie, and the Holy Spirit,

I took today off from work. While I was out in the flower garden, I saw this little red thing glinting up at me. I had already raked this area last evening, but I looked more closely and I saw that this thing glinting at me was a shiny plastic heart in the dirt! A heart! A heart in the dirt, in the ground, just like Grace said: "I will be close to you by the flowers and the ground!" Thank you, sweetheart! It really made my day! Please realize that all this helps me to understand and to see! You know that I need encouragement now, so that really means so much. Thank you for this love!

I seem to be wondering what to do now. Amanda told me earlier that she wanted me to go to her dance rehearsal tonight, but now she is with her mother and has not called to tell me where or when it is. But maybe I can use this time to read or something. Dad just came home, Grace, and he seems to be in a bad mood, so I will just be who I am. Help me to send love to him.

Mother, you try so hard. Do not deny your humanness. This also makes you who you are. Be, dearest. Just be. This will assist you in this new phase of life. You are full of love, so be full of love. You sense the energy of my father and this frightens you, because you feel you cannot be as you are. This is not true! You can be who you are at all times. Think, now, of how beautiful things can be for you. And then you will be there. You need not take on anyone else's energy as if it were your own.

I have done this for a long time, have I not?

Yes! You will see. Mother, taking on other people's energy has injured you in the past. But you will see. This lesson has crossed your path for a specific reason.

What can I do, Grace?

Be human. Know this is fine. Let this show. You need not argue if you feel this would not benefit you. Just be, dearest. Calm will come. The quiet will come. Do something for yourself. My father needs his space and time. Do something for yourself!

Okay, I will. I think I will go to my mother's for the night. Amanda has not called. I will see you—I mean, write to you—soon.

April 24, 1996

Dearest Grace, Trinity, the Angels, and the Holy Spirit,

Hello! I am back at home and feeling much better. Thank you. I went to my mother's and actually got a great sleep there. It was so needed. I came home and John was still somewhat in a tizzy about things, but I was able to not let this affect me. I thank you again.

Mother, you took such good care of yourself last night. We know how easy it would have been to defend your position in all of this. The spirit was with you and you acted with it. See how easy this can be when you follow your heart? This has been revealed to you. Mother, when you see, you respond and you show the world how things can be with spirit. With knowing. With humanness.

Grace, I am feeling so much more comfortable about talking to you. I want you to know this. Having you in my life is so important, and to know that we are not really separated means even more. I think that I have crossed some type of line in belief. That I know we are together. I treasure this.

Our love has always been so very strong, my Mother. These bonds are not created overnight, so to speak. This has been proven throughout time. We came to human form to show, to reveal, this love. And it has been revealed through you and me. Know that we love with totality, with pureness, from both our hearts. Stop and know that our love has been with you since you were a little girl. You have heard my voice and I yours, through time.

Thank you, Grace. Thank you for your guidance tonight and last night. You knew just what to do. I feel that I need help when I am changing my behavior and showing it in more loving ways. You know that I have a problem with being human and all that, and also with being a perfectionist.

You are doing fine! We know that you will do all that needs to be done. And we, of course, will be there should you need any of us. If you have any questions, you know where to turn, do you not?

Yes, I do. In thanks, I say this. It takes me a little time sometimes with this. To have it all penetrate. Well, darling girl, good night.

Good night, Mama, good night.

Good night, Trinity, my sweet angel guardian.

Gracie,   April 27, 1996

   Can we talk?

Always, Mother. I am here for you. I love that you want to be so close to me during these times when we are so connected. I thank you for these times, my dear Mother. You are blessed with these times. I want you to know this.

Thank you, Gracie. The blessing is in that we are together through time, that this can even take place. I don't want you to feel left out when I struggle with things, because you are always in my heart. There is not a day that goes by in which I do not think of you in some way. It has been hard for me to understand how I can do this. How I can talk to you after so many months when I never heard your voice. But I am so grateful. You see, I cry every time we talk because I miss you so. I think that you would have been almost two, and we could have gone out today and raked or something, or you could have run errands with me.

I know that you are in spirit form, but sometimes it is just plain hard for me. I have seen two newborns recently, and I get all welled up. I thought this would be such a perfect time to be a mother, such a good time of life for me. I am older and more settled down, and I have gone through a transformation of sorts. I like myself better, or at least understand myself better, but it gets tough. I am running out of time. I know I do have Amanda. I do not know what I would do without her.

I guess I simply miss you, honey. My mother said the other day how beautiful you were. And you were. Just a perfect child. So you see, I do live in two worlds. The one of knowing you as you were and the one of knowing you now in spirit. I am so glad that I have something of you. My mind is wanting to catch up to the rest of me, to my heart. I want you to know these things, dearest.

I say to you, my dear, dear Mother. Live! I want you to live! I want you to be in life. It is an honor that you remember me, a tremendous honor. But I want you to live. Participate! You look back and say, "But what if this?" or "What if that?" I say, live! All of life gives you wonder. With or without me in physical form, you will still have wonder in your life. Treasure these moments because they bring you closer to me. We are together now! We dwell in these moments together. I am in your heart. In the perfection of God's love for you! You look to the past, dear Mother. It is time to look at what is right in front of you. LIVE! BE! CELEBRATE THIS WONDER!

I do, Grace. I want to live. I thought I was living, that I am always living. I thought that I felt the wonder of things. That . . .

Mother, feel the wonder of this. Feel that you are speaking to me NOW! That we are together NOW. Feel this. Please feel this!

Gracie, have I been denying that you were in spirit form?

Mother, this is right in front of you—this wonder. You can choose to believe whatever you choose. But you know this. I am here for you, telling you, from the arms of God, that all is well. That all is as it should be. I am here. Right here. What holds you back, dear one? You can examine this.

Grace, help me to believe this. I do, and then my mind gets all funny on me. I talk to you here, and then I doubt at times. Why?

Mother, you cry tears when we speak. You are moved by feeling. You are moved by love, the love of the words that are so close to you, in thought, with me. This is belief.

You have felt this love for so long. It is in looking at what Is that you are having a miscommunication. This IS! I was always more spirit than human in form. This is the reality! Spirit is the reality, dearest! When you are most true to yourself, it is in spirit that you are able to realize this.

You say, "But the body, what of the body?" Well, what of the body? You struggle with the concept of the body. You struggle with what is not seen, may not be real. But you know.

You know that love is not seen. Trinity is not seen. Thoughts are not seen. But there is belief that all of these exist. The material world brings only that which is material. The spirit world brings that of the spirit. You are crossing into that which cannot be seen. This is a marvel! You struggle with what was once seen and is no longer seen through the physical eyes.

Because you have known me in physical form as a child, you ask now, can it be both? Yet realize the essence is always there, dear Mother, our love is always there. If you hold that close to you, you will see. You will see that it does not matter in which form we come together, be it spirit or physical.

Gracie, thank you. I know you are with me. Thank you for being so patient with a mother who loves you so and yet struggles with this reality. I will hold our love in my heart and let it guide me. I can really see when I keep that in focus. Thank you for that. Can you fill me with your love?

We could not be talking here, my dearest, if our love lights, our spirits, had not combined as one. You are filled with love! Do not fret, nor worry. Live! Be! Let this day be filled with a happiness you have never known. Mother, realize how special you truly are. That is all I will say. How truly special you are!

Grace, I feel almost drowsy now. Thank you. I think that I will rest.

Dearest Grace,   April 1996

I come to you tonight because I don't know what else to do. All my thoughts center on what is happening here—right here at the computer. I don't know how to say this, but I am having such a hard time with all of this. I feel as if what little faith I had in all that has transpired is ebbing away or being challenged. I come, Grace, once again, with despair in my heart.

You are my daughter, first and foremost in my mind. I have had to understand things I never thought I would. First your life, then your death, and now your life again.

I have to tell you this, because from the first I trusted you as I have never trusted anyone. You were a miracle to me. And now I question how this can even be happening. How is this possible?

Grace, first I had to get my mind around the computer that glowed, then a computer that scrolled with shimmering letters, then a computer that would not write—all of this is part of my physical world. And God knows, I have had feelings every inch of the way with this, but I have accepted it.

When I asked if you would come to me before, I thought it might be in a dream or vision. I have had to understand your death, Grace, and now you ask me to understand your life. I ask myself if this would be easier for me if you had died as an adult and this had happened? But you were my baby. Gracie, I have had to go through so much with your death, so much pain. I cannot stay away—I have to write to you. But how far can a human mind stretch?

I ask myself why. When I read Peace's words or hear Trinity's voice, I don't doubt. Is it because they are more abstract to me? Gracie, I look at Margaret and see her faith in the angels and God, and I admire her faith so much. Then I sit here and wonder how this can be possible. Please forgive me, darling.

When I heard your voice that first night, it was as if I were remembering a conversation of yesterday and recalling the voices of my sister or mother—there was that much of a distinction between your voice and Trinity's. I cried so hard that night, sweetheart, I had to hang on to the computer—I even kissed the screen. But Gracie, I have stretched more than I ever wanted to. More than I ever believed was possible. I pray to you, to everyone who can help me to understand, if it is possible, please help me to see how this can be. I know you are an angel—I know this. I just never thought it would be this way. I thought that you would have wings or something, that I could see you. Darling, please forgive me. You were my baby—I mean are my baby. Don't you understand? I'm even having a hard time trying to put these words on paper. I guess I don't even know what to call you, angel or daughter. I believe in the spirit—I just never thought it would be quite this way.

Dear Angels, Trinity, and Gracie,   May 1, 1996
I got up out of bed tonight. This crisis in belief continues. Why is this? Can you help me with this? I am doubting everything. Everything. How can this be happening? Why is this? Please, if this is for the highest good . . .

Mama, I stand by you. Thank you for coming tonight to speak with us.
You hear the words to the music on now: "Two branches of one tree.
God bless our love." Is this not so? You worry so about faith and yet you
turn to us when in doubt. This is the truest faith there can be. You turn
to me and have since the moment of my birth, in faith and love. How
you have trusted this love! And so blessed is this love! Oh, Mother, if I
could only make you see. It is for you to realize. But let me tell you that
you will see! That this will bring you to such a place of comfort. Your
honesty brings you to such a place of knowing. This you can trust. This
trueness, even in the face of doubt, is what we speak of here. Your being
true to self shows that you believe in who you are, that you have the
courage to be who you are! Even in doubt, you are who you are! Oh,
Mother of mine, celebrate this huge step. Once again, you trust who
you are! Do you not see that you can see? Now sleep. I will be with
you. I love and adore you so.

Dear Angels and Grace,   May 1996

I worked in the yard tonight. I keep hoping that something will come to me. If I have a problem, I have to get outside to sort it out.

I have worried constantly, Grace, about this situation, about hearing your voice. I don't know where to turn.

In my dream of last night I saw a file cabinet. In the drawer that was open was a file labeled "Effort." The scene switched rapidly, to my looking at a female physician bending over a child, an infant. I was looking at the doctor from behind. She was caring for this child, and I could sense that she was very desperate. I kept watching this scene. When she turned to look at me, I saw in anguish that she was me. I saw that my eyes had welled with tears. I saw the deep pain in my eyes and my heart just broke. Have I been trying to save you, Grace? What have I done to myself? God help me. . . .

Dearest Gracie and Trinity,   May 2, 1996

I woke up today feeling out of sorts. This crisis continues. What is going on? Is it because I have doubted? Is it because I do not know who I am? Who am I, anyway? I feel like just a body now, as if I have no past, present, or future.

Mother, thank you for coming and wanting to communicate again in this time. You struggle and yet there is no struggle. There is nothing to worry about. I do not want to diminish your perceptions, but this is illusion. You find yourself in this place—this place of questions. Have you not asked questions before? Have you not become someone new before? Did you not move from singleness to a married state with my father? Did you not move from childlessness to motherhood with Amanda? Have you not questioned before? This is what this is about. Questions. And it is as it should be. It is fine to question who you are, who you might want to become. In spirit form, you are always timeless. You question now what it is on the physical plane.

But Gracie, have I ever known who I was, or was I just pretending? Did I think I knew who I was when I really did not?

You question now with honesty. This is something you had a more

212

difficult time doing in the past. Now you want to be who you are and this feels foreign to you. This is that feeling of emptiness that has arisen. Yet you breathe easier. Do you not find this interesting?

Grace, I find this interesting and somewhat hopeful. Please know that I believe in you but this place is difficult for me. I know that you see so clearly and, in your eyes, I probably have muddled vision. Yet this seems big, some-how, to me. Can you just bear with me?

Thank you for all that I have. Even if I doubt, I want you to know that you are the best thing that could have happened to me. So I will just trust that all will be fine, somehow. Okay? I have to go to work. Simply, thanks. I am just so very confused.

May 1996

Dearest Angels, Trinity, Gracie, and the Holy Spirit,

I ask now that you help me with these letters to you, Grace. I ask that you help me with this confusion, this disbelief I struggle with. . . . And yet this love in my heart, this love for you, Grace, is so real. I feel this, this realness.

Mother, thank you. It is with honor that we see the love on these pages and know that this lies within your dear heart. This will free you. This writing will free you. Your breathing comes with ease now. This is so reflective of what IS. Do you not feel the lightness coming into being? I am close to you now. Very close. You feel my energy. My light. We are as one as we speak here. We have been as one inhabiting the same body, the same energy. Feel strong in this knowing. You may write now.

KNOWING

Dearest Grace,   June 1996

You know that I have been struggling with my faith, with trying to understand all of this. I had to run to write to you this morning, because I woke up with an intense sense of relief. I know that I dreamed of having faith— that what I felt I lacked was already there. But thoughts are rushing from me even now as I write. I realize that I could not have faith or believe in all of this unless I felt I *knew* what it meant. The Greeks have a word called *gnosis,* meaning "self-knowledge" or "self-knowing." I kept getting hung up on *what* things meant—the questions—

rather than what I *knew*. First let me define *knowing* as "perceiving or understanding clearly and with certainty."

Let me try to explain. On a very basic level, through *physical* union, your father and I *knew* each other, and we had you. We *united* by *knowing* each other. This *uniting* happens all the time. Even with thought. For instance, when someone understands an idea, he or she may say, "I get it!" meaning the person *sees* and *understands clearly* and with *certainty*. To do this one must first *unite* with this idea. The idea becomes a part of that person. You *become* the idea through *uniting* with it.

I united with you as a mother *physically*. I *knew* you as a mother. However, I resisted the idea that you, as an angel, were in spirit form. To me, you were still my baby. Yet, you were teaching me that if I could come to *know*, to *see*, to *understand* and *perceive* reality, I could unite with you in spirit.

When I *knew* you in spirit, Grace, I *knew* God. When I *knew* God, I *knew* my *self*. I somehow became united. How many times did Trinity tell me I *knew*? This was my key to unlocking the part of me that had become confused. But let me go on.

Grace, I have tried my whole life to control outcomes. I did this by being good, or trying to be good. When you died and I could not control that, I reasoned that my worst fear had been revealed—I somehow was bad. I justified your death by making myself wrong, and to be wrong you must be flawed. I viewed death as a punishment, the final scene, often painful and full of loss. Then the events began happening.

First, let's look at the comforter being tucked around me. I *knew* when this occurred that it had something to do with you. I never questioned that. I just *knew*. If one were to comfort a loved one, tucking them in bed would be such a gentle indication of this. It worked. I was comforted. Then there was the glowing computer—once again, I *knew* that this had to do with you. The computer had never glowed before you were born, and I only used it to write to you. This is the *one way* I could feel close to you. It was our *connection*. I *knew* this.

Next, your father told me to be *natural* about my out-of-body experience—that it was nothing bad. This opened me up to seeing *(knowing)* that if I was *out* of my body, then my real self was something other than my body. If not a body, then what? I kept stumbling into answers revolving around the spirit. Or *was* I stumbling?

We now come to the aspect of the computer scrolling. I was so deeply affected by this event that I literally fell to my knees and prayed—and I was crying. This was more than a knee-jerk reaction, that of praying. It was something I *knew* in the deepest part of me to do, like breathing. I think now of other men and women who have fallen to their knees when touched by the divine. No one teaches you that. You do it because it feels natural, because you *know*.

Grace, when I think of the burning bush that Moses saw, the tree that bloomed in the dead of winter for St.

216

Francis, I realize that these experiences happened using familiar landscapes to convey divine messages within the *physical* world. The computer was *my* landscape and a means for me to connect to you in my mind and heart. What had I witnessed? And how had I *known* so completely that this was divine?

Yet, my mind kept telling me to reason. Figure it out. More questions, always questions. *Why? How? It is not possible,* were all familiar thoughts. What we do not understand, we fear. This fear kept cropping up for me. It was an illusion that kept me in a state of confusion. When you hang your hat on illusion, it becomes impossible to *see* love. This fear is now gone.

I reasoned that divine experiences were only for others. That I somehow was not qualified to *know*, to see clearly. I was not holy. I was way too ordinary—and bad at that. But events kept occurring, each ultimately revealing a message of love.

I was open to angelic communication—to the messages of Peace and the teachings, in my case, of Trinity. I began slowly to heal through Trinity's words and to *know* myself. I began to *see* and *understand*. Yet, these angels remained somewhat abstract, seen as divine messengers coming from another place.

When I *heard* your voice, Grace, I went into another tailspin. I trusted what I *saw* on the computer, such as the crosses, shimmering letters, as being more valid than what I *heard*—your voice. I kept trying to reason that a baby could not talk, that you were still my baby. I was playing by earthly rules and chronological age—you were telling me there was a much larger way of looking at my life, that spirit is ageless. Although I *knew* what I had heard, I kept waffling. My mind told me I could not be truly faithful if I questioned.

Grace, you could never remain abstract for me—ever. Once again, for a person such as myself, the fact that you came to me as you did shows me how the divine is at work. You have been the single most altering experience of my life, and I have never loved more. God *knew* that. You *knew* that. And I *knew* that.

This was revealed to me through you. I kept hanging on to the thought that you had died. And with that, a part of me died. But you encouraged me to live.

My abstract view of angels and all things holy was reinforced by seeing God as something distant and far away. I saw heaven as a place to go to rather than a state of being. With you in my heart, I realize God is there also. But the real miracle is that I have moved somehow to seeing God as *living,* because of your continued life in spirit.

I see so clearly that what I know, I *knew* all along.

Grace, you have become my doorway. Seeing your divinity, I *knew* God not as something out there, but as alive and working in my life. And through you, I have been able to see my own divinity, as coming from my humanity, from acceptance, love, and forgiveness. What began as a baby journal now has become a type of prayer book for me. These letters really are prayers to God, through you and through Trinity.

I see how my dreams were my gateways to comprehending and integrating lost aspects of myself. They assisted with this vision, giving me comfort all the way. I see how I used them as my guideposts toward a deeper understanding.

I see so much now. I see this great plan at work. Almost as if it were some great dance, everyone having a part. I see how both Margaret and Julie were not coincidences in my life; that both of them, each with her own brand of love, entered my life for a reason. Margaret, who was the first to speak to an angel, was a writer and could capture divine messages beautifully on paper; she helped open another door. She was the first to see these letters to you, and she told me immediately that these letters were beautiful and needed to be shared so that they could help others. I see that if the computer had been operating correctly, I would not have even asked Margaret for help, nor you, later in my prayers.

I see Julie as having opened my heart with her incredible tenderness and *feeling,* and propelling me to a place of forgiveness. I could have shut down forever. But she became my greatest comfort. Each of these women had a part in this story—this healing. Each of us became *united* somehow with our own particular spiritual journeys. And somehow we had created a kind of "church" by sharing our lives.

I see your father having the strength and understanding that I so desperately needed. Our marriage may not have survived had it not been for him. I could have run away as I had from so much in life and hid from myself. I see how he encouraged me to be *natural,* and that spirit is the *natural* state of being. I see Amanda drawing me out of this shell, this armor that I had surrounded myself with, telling me to live as you were—it is all so perfect.

I see my mother as the ultimate listener—always giving of herself when I called, crying. I see my father, after I told him that I was talking to an angel, as telling me that I should always "follow my heart." I see your Grandma Love, who probably never believed that I would end up speaking to angels, sending me an angel book after you died, causing me to *look* in that direction. Everyone had a divine role. Each member of the family, each friend.

I see now how I thought I was in control. I awkwardly thought that I could control aspects of my life by *trying* harder with everything. This was revealed in my continuing conversations with Trinity. How can one *see* anything if one is always *trying?*

I had put myself in a state of perpetual deprivation. This was my ultimate illusion. I had a false sense of security that kept me emotionally and spiritually deficient and exhausted. For years this has been such a burden to me. I thought that *everything* rested on my shoulders, that I rose and fell with how much effort I put into things. I release this to you Grace—to God. It is such a relief.

I see how the pain of your death also kept me grappling in some type of emotional desert. I saw only pain. I was tied to the pain. I had *united* with the idea of pain and therefore lashed out at myself to create my own personal prison. As Trinity told me continually, you can choose to think what you want. I had chosen hell, because I thought that was the only choice available. And yet, you were merely moving from one state to another in love— *painlessly.*

Just as we can be connected to someone here on earth through pain, we can also be connected to someone in spirit through pain. If I really believed in your *death,* how could I then believe in your *continued life in spirit?* This pain was erased when I realized that you actually lived. This seems miraculous to me.

In reality, it is our love that remains constant. That was what you were trying to tell me. I *know* this now, Grace. I also see how this *knowing* has always been a part of me. That this knowing was my faith, *even if* I questioned.

Grace, I see these ripples coming out from my heart, from all of this. I see how we all love our children, wanting safety and beauty for them, within their hearts. I know now that you are safe and that you have found the beauty you sought. I see that this is what God wants for all of us: safety, love, and beauty.

Gracie, I think that I am on the path. I really believe that everyone in the human condition has come to the earth to learn how to love, that we are all visitors for a short while, and then we leave. In reality, we are somehow more than our bodies; we are all of the spirit. For me, it is so comforting to *know* that there is no pain in death.

I see now that you did not need to stay any longer than you did. Your life was complete—even at five weeks. You did what you came to do, what you were meant to do. I say this in humbleness. When I see how you have honored me by loving me so deeply, by coming to me to show me only love, this alone moves me to a place of profound gratefulness.

Thank you, darling, for this message of love. I have the courage now to be who I am, as I am. I know now that everything is possible.

EPILOGUE:
INTEGRATING

A door opened, and I went through it. That door was communication. I moved from a place of disbelief to a place of total knowing in my communication with Grace. I walked through this door only because of my love for Grace. Grace and I have continued to speak to one another and I have continued to heal.

The lessons I learned from Trinity and Grace became integrated into who I was. For so long, so much of my life surrounding the birth and death of my daughter had centered on loss. And so much of my healing revolved around finding. These concepts appeared as separate entities for me. Loss had entered my life as some savage intruder that destroyed all that I loved. Finding Grace became a balm that healed my wounds.

However, one question still lingered in the back of my mind. I did not realize this until I turned the key in my back door one day and had a memory of Amanda asking if she could talk to me one night, two months after Grace had died. I told her yes, and she crawled into bed with me where I had been reading. Amanda was having difficulty asking me whatever she needed to know but finally she simply said, "Did Gracie die because of me?"

I was astonished. Amanda went on to say that she thought Grace had died because of a story she had read to her in the hospital! Tears stung my eyes. I told her no, this was impossible. She asked how I knew. I told her I was Grace's mother, and mothers always know. I told her that Gracie had been sick and it was no one's fault. I held Amanda and felt that familiar wooden feeling grow in me again. What I did not realize was that I, too, was asking the same question about myself.

I realized all of this as I turned the key in our back door, two and a half years after my daughter's death. As I turned the key I heard the words: "You are absolved." I felt jolted into a new reality. I saw how ridiculous it was for Amanda to have felt that way, and yet I understood in her humanness how she could ask this. I knew then that this is how God saw me—as a child asking a question for which I was sure guilt and fear were the only answers.

These were the exact illusions that Trinity and Grace had spoken of: guilt and fear. I saw the impossibility of what had driven me for months. I had brought light into fear. And fear dissolved into thin air.

I realized how shame and guilt were so closely tied to loss. It became so clear for me. When we say, "I lost my temper," "I lost my job," "I lost my child," what are we really saying? The implication here is that if something is lost, it is gone and cannot be found. But by the same token, is finding not the opposite of losing? So often we stop at loss and believe that is all there is. What we had is gone. We totally blew it. Our chance is gone. We do not perceive of the connection, the lesson of duality that Trinity and Grace both spoke of.

We divide completion, or the ability to heal, when we think in terms of opposites—and therefore we extinguish the opportunity and potential for uniting and becoming whole within ourselves. We say what is lost cannot be found. We stop at loss, because we do not believe that being found is part of the same equation. But are loss and finding not one and the same? Is the circle not the beginning and the ending at the same time? Is this not the exact lesson, or way of seeing, that unifies rather than separates and destroys? We do not believe at the time of loss that what we seek is there.

This is exactly what the concept of duality does to us. It separates instead of unifies. I am sinner or blessed, up or down, straight or crooked. But reality is not this way. In the union of what appeared to be in opposition to itself, I found love. When I lost, I found. Pure and simple. It was there all the time, the whole while. When I said that Grace had died, I had no idea that I—or God—would be found, let alone Grace. I had no idea that being found was part of losing.

This is the message Grace left me, to see in terms of wholeness, not division. To love all of me, not surgically remove any of who I am. This is the greatest connection that there may be.

FINDING PEACE

I cannot part from these pages without telling one more story from my journey. On November 1, 1996, which happened to be All Saints' Day, my husband John and I went out to dinner. We were talking about the miracle of this book and how it could even have come to be—simply from letters to our daughter.

For some reason, John, who has never asked anything of me, asked, "Can you write about Grace's death; can you put that in the book?" I got tears in my eyes and said, "John, tell me what it was like." John began to speak softly and slowly, never hesitating. I began to cry as he told me this last part of the story. . . .

"Grace was in my arms. She had her little fingers wrapped around my thumb—just like Amanda used to do when she was little. I was in the rocking chair with her. And then it was as if time expanded into some great arch and Grace went into it. She simply moved into this place. There was total silence, and yet the room was filled. I had just been speaking to your father about why people have to suffer as Grace did. And then she was gone. I knew that God had heard me. I was so amazed that God had listened. It was so beautiful, and such a great honor to be there. . . ."

I was crying so hard. This was such a gift to me, to hear these words. John held my hand and neither of us spoke. I hung on to John's words. This was the only memory I have of Grace's death to cling to, because I had not been there.

I could not shake the feeling of that evening. It stayed with me the whole next day. That night, I asked Grace about it, still needing to hear. I finally had the courage to ask.

This is my last gift of Grace to you, the words of her death. . . .

My father, John, was holding me in his arms. There was no pain and no greater safety. My father spoke of suffering. He was telling my grandfather of my suffering. At the time, I wondered why, for I felt no pain. I knew this to be how they felt suffering in their hearts. My mother's spirit was with me all the while. She could be in spirit form only in a dream state, and so she came to me, to help me, as she felt she slept.

It was all predestined to be like this, that she slept while I left the physical world. This was not meant to bring grief, but to have her close to me. It could only be done as she slept.

My father's words of suffering were heard by God, for there is no greater appeal than that of a parent. There were many, many angels, many to see me to the higher realms—there was light everywhere. It filled me. It filled the room. It filled my father and grandfather. And yes, there was an arch; this is the passageway I traveled in love. And there were many to greet me, to KNOW me, to celebrate in love!

Time, as my father sensed and my grandfather knew, was nonexistent. We were all out of time, in eternity. We had risen above duality, pain, and fear, and in those moments we touched God.

When my father said that God had heard him, he heard God! And in this he is blessed, as my grandfather is blessed and you, my mother, are blessed.

For mother, it was you who guided me to the light. . . .

And so I leave you here, at the end of this love story. I want all of you to know, in gratitude, what the making of this book has done for me. It has healed the deepest part of my soul and left me so complete. I thank you.

I give you these letters now in love, from Grace, in total peace.

Sincerely,
Mary Kathryn Love

ABOUT THE AUTHOR

Mary Kathryn Love lives in St. Paul, Minnesota, with her husband, stepdaughter, and four cats. She enjoys gardening and conversation, and has a deep appreciation for the quiet solitude that books and reading offer. She grew up in South America and attended high school and college in Minnesota. Love continues to write, having found this to be one of the aspects of life that contains her joy. She is currently a Program Associate in the ISP Executive Study Program at the University of Minnesota. She can be contacted through the web site of The Grace Foundation: http://www.gracezurilovefoundation.com

Hazelden Publishing and Education is a division of the Hazelden Foundation, a not-for-profit organization. Since 1949, Hazelden has been a leader in promoting the dignity and treatment of people afflicted with the disease of chemical dependency.

The mission of the foundation is to improve the quality of life for individuals, families, and communities by providing a national continuum of information, education, and recovery services that are widely accessible; to advance the field through research and training; and to improve our quality and effectiveness through continuous improvement and innovation.

Stemming from that, the mission of the publishing division is to provide quality information and support to people wherever they may be in their personal journeys—from education and early intervention, through treatment and recovery, to personal and spiritual growth.

Although our treatment programs do not necessarily use everything Hazelden publishes, our bibliotherapeutic materials support our mission and the Twelve Step philosophy upon which it is based. We encourage your comments and feedback.

The headquarters of the Hazelden Foundation are in Center City, Minnesota. Additional treatment facilities are located in Chicago, Illinois; New York, New York; Plymouth, Minnesota; St. Paul, Minnesota; and West Palm Beach, Florida. At these sites, we provide a continuum of care for men and women of all ages. Our Plymouth facility is designed specifically for youth and families.

For more information on Hazelden, please call 1-800-257-7800. Or you may access our World Wide Web site on the Internet at http://www.hazelden.org.